THE EXPELLED LAW STUDENT

THE EXPELLED LAW STUDENT
A Case Law Survey

ROBERT M. JARVIS
PROFESSOR OF LAW
NOVA SOUTHEASTERN UNIVERSITY

The Expelled Law Student
A Case Law Survey

Robert M. Jarvis
Professor of Law
Nova Southeastern University

Published by:

Vandeplas Publishing, LLC – November 2022

801 International Parkway, 5th Floor
Lake Mary, FL. 32746
USA

www.vandeplaspublishing.com

ISBN 978-1-60042-546-2

TABLE OF CONTENTS

During my 35 years as a faculty member, I have served on nearly every committee at my law school that has anything to do with student expulsions: the Scholastic Standing Committee (1987-93); the Application Amendments Committee (1993-95); the Student Affairs Committee (1999-2003, 2011-12, 2017-18); the Academic Disciplinary Board (2012-16); the Admissions Committee (2019-21); and, most recently, the *Ad Hoc* Disciplinary Committee (2021-22). I also have filed my fair share of honor court complaints. Without a doubt, having to decide if a law student should be expelled is the worst part of being a law professor.

Over the years, as I went about my duties, I increasingly wondered about other law schools and their expulsion experiences. I also began to wonder about the litigation generated by law school expulsions. In 2013, curiosity finally got the better of me and I began to explore these matters. The result is this little book, which discusses every judicial opinion (through February 28, 2022) I have been able to locate involving an expelled law student. (In the chapter notes, I have added several cases issued between March 1 and June 30, 2022.)

I hope readers will find the present undertaking to be both informative and useful. I also invite them to send comments, corrections, or suggestions to me at jarvisb@nova.edu. In closing, I wish to express my thanks to the publisher's staff; my wife Judi; and my law school colleagues Gail L. Richmond and Debra Moss Vollweiler.

For Dad

The Cleveland, Ohio, gravesite of Harry Koblitz,
the first expelled U.S. law student to bring a readmission lawsuit
(photograph courtesy of Debra L. Dennewitz)

Chapter 1

INTRODUCTION

Law schools typically expel students for one of five reasons: 1) lying to gain admission; 2) financial issues; 3) poor grades; 4) cheating; or 5) inappropriate, dangerous, or criminal behavior.[1]

Being expelled from law school is a devastating experience that often has lifelong consequences.[2] Prior to 1970, however, law students rarely challenged their expulsions in court. In contrast, during the past 50 years such lawsuits have become commonplace, even as the number of law students who annually are expelled has fallen dramatically.[3] Three factors appear to account for this change: 1) a decline in the quality of high school and college instruction, which has left many students unprepared for the rigors of law school;[4] 2) the skyrocketing cost of law school (which has given expelled students more incentive to seek reinstatement);[5] and 3) the enactment of numerous disability anti-discrimination laws, which both has encouraged students with special needs to go to law school and made law schools vulnerable to "failure-to-accommodate" claims.[6] There also, of course, has been a dramatic rise in the number of law schools and law students. In 1970-71, there were 146 ABA-approved law schools and 78,018 law students.[7] In 2020-21, there were 199 ABA-approved law schools and 114,520 law students.[8] This expansion, many believe, has made it easier for unqualified applicants to get into law school.[9]

Somewhat surprisingly, to date no effort has been made to collect in one place all the reported judicial decisions involving expelled law students.[10] Accordingly, this little book seeks to fill the gap. (It is hoped that the fulsome chapter notes and index, which are intended to "flesh out" the text, will be viewed as a boon.) Before proceeding, a few caveats are in order.

First, no claim is made that every law school expulsion case has been located.[11] Instead, all I claim is that I have conducted numerous on-line searches to try to find such cases.[12]

Second, certain types of cases have been excluded. These include: 1) cases in which a law student was threatened with expulsion but ended up receiving a lesser sanction;[13] 2) cases in which a law student was expelled but later was readmitted to his or her law school;[14] 3) cases in which a law student was expelled but later was admitted to another law school;[15] 4) cases in which a law student was not expelled but was denied his or her degree;[16] 5) cases in which a law student's suspension became a *de facto* expulsion;[17] 6) cases in which a law student sought to hold a third party responsible for the damages arising from his or her expulsion;[18] 7) cases in which a party's expulsion from law school is mentioned by the court but plays no role in the decision;[19] and 8) cases involving the expulsion of "conditional" law students.[20] Also excluded are cases in which a law school's decision to deny admission to an applicant takes on some of the trappings of an expulsion.[21]

Third, no attempt has been made to examine or critique the processes law schools use to expel students.[22] Not only is such an undertaking beyond the scope of this book, these types of studies already exist.[23]

Lastly, this book is limited to cases involving U.S. law schools.[24] Schools in other countries also expel law students[25] and sometimes are sued as a result.[26]

1   In 1890, however, the University of Maryland expelled William Ash-'
    bie Hawkins for being Black after it decided to resegregate its law
    school. *See Drawing the Color Line: Negro Students Driven Out of
    the Maryland Law School by the Regents*, DAILY INTER OCEAN (Chi.),
    Sept. 15, 1890, at 2. As a result, Hawkins was forced to complete his
    legal education at Howard University. *See* J. CLAY SMITH, JR., EMAN-
    CIPATION: THE MAKING OF THE BLACK LAWYER, 1844-1944, at 38,
    145 (1999). Many years later, a third-year student named Arnold M.
    Jolivet sued the law school, claiming that he too had been expelled
    for being Black. *See* Jolivet v. Elkins, 386 F. Supp. 261 (D. Md. 1974).
    Finding Jolivet's complaint to be time-barred, the district court dis-
    missed it. *Id.* at 272. Following his expulsion, Jolivet became a lob-
    byist for minority-owned businesses. *See* Jacques Kelly, *Arnold M.
    Jolivet*, BALT. SUN, July 29, 2014, at A10.

2   In 2002, for example, Peter O. Odighizuwa, a student about to be
    expelled from Appalachian Law School for the second time due to
    poor grades, suffered a mental breakdown and went on a shooting
    rampage that left three people dead (Dean L. Anthony Sutin, Profes-
    sor Thomas F. Blackwell, and student Angela D. Dales) and three
    people injured (students Stacey Bean, Rebecca C. Brown, and Mar-
    tha M. Short). *See* Francis X. Clines, *3 Slain at Law School; Student is
    Held*, N.Y. TIMES, Jan. 17, 2002, at A18. Odighizuwa eventually pled
    guilty and was given six consecutive life terms plus 28 years. *See Ex-
    Student Pleads Guilty in Shootings*, N.Y. TIMES, Feb. 28, 2004, at A12.

    In *In re: Wolfe*, 501 B.R. 426 (Bankr. M.D. Fla. 2013), Terence K.
    Wolfe claimed that his life had been ruined by his expulsion from
    law school:

In 1991, [the debtor] enrolled in the night program at George Mason University Law School. The debtor was a Dean's Scholar, the winner of a moot court competition, and named "best oral advocate." He was also the editor of the independent Civil Rights Law Journal. But, in 1995, just six weeks before graduation, the debtor was expelled as a result of an honor code violation. The debtor made inquiries to other law schools, but did not seek admission. Thus, the debtor never graduated from law school and maintains that he has never recovered, either personally or professionally, from the expulsion.

Id. at 429-30 (footnote omitted).

When he was charged with securities fraud for his role in the SAC Capital Advisors hedge fund scandal, Mathew C. Martoma successfully fought to keep prosecutors from telling the jury that he had been expelled from Harvard University's law school for falsifying his law school transcript. According to Martoma, his expulsion was a "source of great embarrassment" and "risk[ed] tainting prospective jurors and biasing them against [him]." *See* United States v. Martoma, No. 12 Cr. 973 (PGG), 2014 WL 4384143, at *13 (S.D.N.Y. Sept. 4, 2014), *aff'd*, 894 F.3d 64 (2d Cir. 2017), *cert. denied*, 139 S. Ct. 2665 (2019). After he was convicted, Martoma unsuccessfully moved for a new trial on the ground that because the evidence of his expulsion had not been kept under seal, as he also had requested, the jury was "presumptively biased" against him. *Id.* at *14. For a further look at Martoma's expulsion from law school, see Sheelah Kolhatkar, Black Edge: Inside Information, Dirty Money, and the Quest to Bring Down the Most Wanted Man on Wall Street 193-201 (2017).

In *In re* Promisco, 625 B.R. 715 (Bankr. N.D. Ill. 2021), Joseph J. Promisco was expelled from DePaul University's law school after being convicted of various sex offenses. Forced to take a series of low-paying jobs, he sought to discharge his student loans, which totaled $244,000. In denying his request, the court wrote: "Plaintiff was a law student who knew or had to know that his conduct could result not only in a criminal conviction but also be a bar to obtaining a license to practice law, and that this would negatively affect his financial situation." *Id.* at 732. For a case in which an expelled UCLA law student was granted hardship relief, see *In re* Nanton-Marie, 303 B.R. 228 (Bankr. S.D. Fla. 2003) (the court justified its decision in part by explaining, *id.* at 232, "If we go back to when Debtor was 44, and was kicked out of UCLAW[,] 13 years have passed, a period well beyond the loan repayment.").

Unsurprisingly, the problems experienced by expelled law students have provided fodder for both authors and screenwriters. In the 2001 MTV made-for-TV movie *Spring Break Lawyer*, for example, Jay Garvey (played by Brad Raider) is expelled from law school after he goofs off in class. In dismissing him, Professor Kingston (played by Shashawnee Hall) exclaims: "Mr. Garvey! While I'm sure you'll spend much of your life in a courtroom, I highly doubt it will be as a lawyer! Good-bye Mr. Garvey!" For a further look at the movie, see *Spring Break Lawyer Reviews*, TV GUIDE, *at* https://www.tvguide.com/movies/spring-break-lawyer/review/2030127693/ (last visited Apr. 1, 2022). In Amy Meyerson's novel *The Imperfects* (2020), the principal character is Beck Miller. Having been kicked out of law school for lying on her admission application, she finds herself working as a paralegal and drowning in debt. *Id.* at 83-84, 328, 347-48. In the 2020 Polish movie *The Hater*, a Warsaw University junior law student named Tomasz Giemza (played by Maciej Musiałowski) is expelled for plagiarism and ends up becoming a dangerous social media troll. *See* Sheena Scott, *'The Hater' on Netflix: The Sinister Consequences to Social Media Trolling*, FORBES, July 30, 2020, *at* https://www.forbes.com/sites/sheenascott/2020/07/30/the-hater-on-netflix-the-sinister-consequences-to-social-media-trolling/?sh=3c0a71cb4bb2. *See also* DIANNE DRAKE, LILLY's LAW (2004), a romance novel that involves a traffic court judge named Lilly Malloy. While she was a law student, Malloy was expelled after her lover (Mike Collier) accused her of plagiarism (the charges were dropped, and Malloy was readmitted, after Collier recanted). *Id.* at 20-21. Years later, Malloy seeks revenge when Collier is hauled into her courtroom for failing to pay nineteen parking tickets. *Id.* at 7-8. Predictably, the pair fall back in love. *Id.* at 218. Similarly, in Lee Stockdale's novel *Murder of Law* (2007), William J. "Billy" Burns is expelled from prestigious Blackstone Law School after he is framed for plagiarism. *Id.* at 48-52. He is reinstated, however, after he exposes the plotters. *Id.* at 199-203.

In an unusual example of life imitating art, Daryl Elfield, a Washington and Lee University law student, missed class to pursue a romance with a stranger he had met on a train. Elfield recently had seen the movie *Before Sunrise* (1995), in which two strangers meet on a train and fall in love. Upon returning to school, Elfield told his professor he had been sick. When his deception came to light, he was expelled for lying. Elfield subsequently wrote to movie critic Roger Ebert about his misadventure. Years later, Ebert tracked him down for an update and Elfield reported that he was living in London and studying to become a barrister. *See* Roger Ebert, *London Calling, and It's Daryl*, ROGEREBERT.COM, Dec. 12, 2004, *at* https://www.rogerebert.com/answer-man/london-calling-and-its-daryl.

Like Elfield, most law students manage to rebuild their lives after being dismissed. In 1955, John V. Schappi was expelled from Cornell University's law school after being arrested twice for engaging in lewd conduct in the men's dormitory during alcoholic blackouts. In an essay penned in 2014, Schappi recalled:

> At the time of my expulsion, it felt like the worst thing in the world had just happened. How wrong I was.
>
> I wouldn't have been happy or successful as a practicing attorney. I went to law school mainly because I didn't know what else to do. . . .

Within a month of being expelled, I was working in Washington, DC, as a legal editor at the Bureau of National Affairs (BNA). I wrote headnotes summarizing court rulings and NLRB cases. . . . Soon enough, I fell in love with Washington, with BNA, and with a colleague there who would eventually become my wife.

I stayed at BNA for 40 years [and] enjoyed a satisfying, rewarding career. . . .

John Schappi, *Learning to Live with Adversity Allowed Me to Look Differently at Aging*, AGINGCARE, *at* https://www.agingcare.com/articles/learning-to-live-with-adversity-allowed-me-to-look-differently-at-aging-165681.htm (last visited Apr. 1, 2022).

Following her 2001 expulsion from Hamline University's law school for poor grades, Alaina R. Alexander created a web site called "DismissedLawStudent.com," see Alaina Alexander, *Turning a Setback into a Comeback*, HACK WRITERS, Sept. 2002, *at* https://www.hackwriters.com/dismissedlawstudent.htm; published an audiobook titled *Dismissed Law Student Essays* (2004), *available at* https://www.amazon.com/Dismissed-Student-Essays-Alaina-Alexander/dp/0975853317; and went on to have a career as a contract analyst. *See Alaina Alexander*, LINKEDIN, *at* https://www.linkedin.com/in/alainaalexander510b982/ (last visited Apr. 1, 2022) (reporting that she currently is pursuing an M.L.S. (Master of Legal Studies) degree at the University of Oklahoma's law school).

In 2017, Lamarr Martin was expelled from Georgia State University's law school for poor grades. Martin returned to his job in the campus mailroom and in 2019 was readmitted to the law school. *See* Mara Thompson, *Lamarr Martin Delivers Fresh Outlook on Second Chances*, GEORGIA STATE NEWS HUB, Apr. 16, 2020, *at* https://news.gsu.edu/2020/04/16/lamarr-martin-delivers-fresh-outlook-on-second-chances/. While waiting to reapply, Martin created a YouTube channel chronicling his efforts to determine where he had gone wrong. *Id.* In July 2020, Martin started a company called Law

Student Encourager, LLC to "[p]rovide academic and mental resilience coaching to national and international law students desiring to strategically bounce back from unsatisfactory grades in a semester, placed on academic probation, or academically dismissed from law school." *See Lamarr Martin,* LINKEDIN, *at* https://www.linkedin.com/in/lamarr-martin-085588212/.

3 At one time, law schools routinely admitted enormous freshmen classes and then culled them at the end of the year. This process was so brutal that law school deans typically advised students at orientation to "look to your left and then to your right—one of you won't be here next year." *See, e.g.,* J. Gordon Hylton, *Look to Your Left, Then Look to Your Right: Marquette University Law School, Fall 1919,* MARQUETTE UNIVERSITY LAW SCHOOL FACULTY BLOG, Dec. 9, 2010, *at* https://law.marquette.edu/facultyblog/2010/12/look-to-your-left-then-look-to-your-right-marquette-university-law-school-fall-1919/ ("At almost every law school founded before 1960, a story is told about a past dean who addressed incoming classes by telling them: 'Look to your left and then to your right, and three years from now, only one of you will still be here.' The softer version of the story ended 'and only two of you will still be here.'")

Today, the accreditation rules governing law schools prohibit mass culling. *See* AMERICAN BAR ASSOCIATION SECTION OF LEGAL EDUCATION AND ADMISSIONS TO THE BAR, 2021-2022 STANDARDS AND RULES OF PROCEDURE FOR APPROVAL OF LAW SCHOOLS 31 (2021) [hereinafter ABA LAW SCHOOL STANDARDS], *available at* https://www.americanbar.org/groups/legal_education/resources/standards/ (under Standard 501 ("Admissions"), which states in paragraph (b): "A law school shall only admit applicants who appear capable of satisfactorily completing its program of legal education and being admitted to the bar."). Nevertheless, in 2006 Thomas J. Bentey, who had been expelled from St. Thomas University's law school for poor grades, accused the school of "illegally accepting and then expelling more than 25% of its first-year class to boost its flagging bar pass rates." *See* Leigh Jones, *St. Thomas Law School Sued Over Dismissal Rate*, Miami Daily Bus. Rev., Sept. 5, 2006, at 17. Bentey dropped his lawsuit a few months later. *See* Bentey v. St. Thomas Univ. Sch. of L., No. 1:07-cv-20085-DLG (S.D. Fla.) (stipulation of dismissal dated Apr. 18, 2007), *available at* 2007 WL 1525763.

Because of the ABA's rules, expulsions now are rare. It is impossible to be more precise because no entity tracks law school expulsions. *See* E-mail from Kenneth R. Williams, Senior Data Analyst, Section of Legal Education and Admissions to the Bar—American Bar Association, to the author, dated Feb. 28, 2022, at 5:34 p.m. (copy on file with the author). Although law schools are required to report to the ABA how many students they "attrit" each year, the questionnaire does not specifically ask about expulsions. *See* ABA Section of Legal Education and Admissions to the Bar, *Standard 509 Information Reports* [hereinafter *509 Reports*], *at* https://www.abarequireddisclosures.org/Disclosure509.aspx (last visited Apr. 1, 2022) (under "Compilation—All Schools Data, Attrition"). For a further discussion, see Evan Jones, *Law School Dropout Rates*, Lawschooli, updated Feb. 9, 2022, *at* https://lawschooli.com/law-school-dropout-rates/.

4   Numerous commentators have noted this fact and offered various solutions. *See, e.g.,* Nathan A. Preuss, *Applying Motivation Theory to Improve 1Ls' Motivation, Self-Efficacy, and Skill Mastery*, 114 Law Libr. J. 59 (2022); Laura P. Graham, *Generation Z Goes to Law School: Teaching and Reaching Law Students in the Post-Millennial Generation*, 41 U. Ark. Little Rock L. Rev. 29 (2018); Patti Alleva & Jennifer A. Gundlach, *Learning Intentionally and the Metacognitive Task*, 65 J. Legal Educ. 710 (2016); Jennifer Cooper, *Smarter Law Learning: Using Cognitive Science to Maximize Law Learning*, 44 Cap. U. L. Rev. 551 (2016); Caroline L. Osborne, *The State of Legal Research Education: A Survey of First-Year Legal Programs, or "Why Johnny and Jane Cannot Research,"* 108 Law Libr. J. 403 (2016); Rebecca Flanagan, *The Kids Aren't Alright: Rethinking the Law Student Skills Deficit*, 2015

BYU Educ. & L.J. 135 (2015); Courtney G. Lee, *Changing Gears to Meet the "New Normal" in Legal Education*, 53 Duq. L. Rev. 39 (2015); Susan Stuart & Ruth Vance, *Bringing a Knife to the Gunfight: The Academically Underprepared Law Student & Legal Education Reform*, 48 Val. U. L. Rev. 41 (2013); Melissa J. Marlow, *It Takes a Village to Solve the Problems in Legal Education: Every Faculty Member's Role in Academic Support*, 30 U. Ark. Little Rock L. Rev. 489 (2008); Cathaleen A. Roach, *Is the Sky Falling? Ruminations on Incoming Law Student Preparedness (and Implications for the Profession) in the Wake of Recent National and Other Reports*, 11 Legal Writing: J. Legal Writing Inst. 295 (2005); Christopher W. Holiman, Comment, *Leaving No Law Student Left Behind: Learning to Learn in the Age of No Child Left Behind*, 58 How. L.J. 195 (2014).

For a useful discussion regarding the decline in the quality of U.S. high school and college education, see J.M. Beach, Can We Measure What Matters Most? Why Educational Accountability Metrics Lower Student Learning and Demoralize Teachers (2021) (blaming the decline on a constellation of factors, including, *id.* at 36, "teachers['] low academic expectations, grade inflation, automatic social promotion, low levels of homework, [and] watered down textbooks[.]").

5   In 1970-71, the yearly median tuition at law schools was $523 (public institutions) and $1,705 (private institutions). *See* Richard L. Abel, American Lawyers 58 (1989). By 2020-21, these numbers had jumped, respectively, to $29,074 and $51,268. *See* Ilana Kowarski, *See the Price, Payoff of Law School Before Enrolling*, U.S. News & World Rep., Mar. 31, 2021, *at* https://www.usnews.com/education/best-graduate-schools/top-law-schools/articles/law-school-cost-starting-salary. As a result of these increases, most law students now must borrow heavily to finance their educations. *See* Scott F. Norberg & Stephanie J. Garcia, *Reducing Debt and Increasing Access to the Profession: An Empirical Study of Graduate Debt at U.S. Law Schools*, 69 J. Legal Educ. 720, 724 (2020) ("The meta-average of the

average amounts borrowed by 2018 law graduates across schools was approximately $115,481. The average of the average amounts borrowed by graduates who attended a private law school was significantly higher than for graduates who attended a public school, $130,373 versus $91,803. The total amount borrowed by class of 2018 graduates was $2.96 billion.").

6   In 1973, Congress passed the Rehabilitation Act (colloquially known as "Section 504"), followed in 1990 by the Americans with Disabilities Act ("ADA"). *See* DORIS ZAMES FLEISCHER *&* FRIEDA ZAMES, THE DISABILITY RIGHTS MOVEMENT: FROM CHARITY TO CONFRONTATION xxvii–xxviii (updated ed. 2011). These statutes, along with their state counterparts, suddenly made law school a realistic option for many disabled students. *See* Jennifer Jolly-Ryan, *Disabilities to Exceptional Abilities: Law Students with Disabilities, Nontraditional Learners, and the Law Teacher as a Learner,* 6 NEV. L.J. 116, 121 (2005) ("Before adoption of Section 504 and the ADA, few students with disabilities were admitted to undergraduate school, and even fewer to law school.").

By 1995, approximately 2% of law students were asking for disability accommodations. *See* Donald Stone, *The Impact of the Americans with Disabilities Act on Legal Education and Academic Modifications for Disabled Law Students: An Empirical Study,* 44 U. KAN. L. REV. 567, 569 n.5 (1996). By 2010, this number had increased to 3.4%. *See* ABA Commission on Mental and Physical Disability Law, *Disability Statistics Report 2011* (Jan. 28, 2011), at 2, *available at* https://www.americanbar.org/content/dam/aba/administrative/market_research/20110314_aba_disability_statistics_report.pdf.

Since the ABA's 2011 report, no further efforts have been made to determine the number of law students with disabilities. *See* Christina Payne-Tsoupros, *A Starting Point for Disability Justice in Legal Education,* 6 J. COMMITTED SOC. CHANGE RACE *&* ETHNICITY 165, 167 (2020) ("There are currently no data capturing the numbers of disabled law students matriculating each year. Data from the U.S.

Department of Education (2019) shows that 11.9% of students in post-baccalaureate programs self-reported a disability in 2015-2016, but that number is not disaggregated by graduate program."). For its part, "[t]he National Association for Law Placement has estimated that between 1 and 2 percent of law school graduates have some sort of disability." Brandon Lowrey, *Will Law Schools Start Counting 'Generation ADA'?*, LAW360, Aug. 16, 2018, *at* https://www.law360.com/articles/1074290. Others, however, believe the actual number is much higher:

> In US law schools today, it is estimated that at least 10 percent of law students have a disability. . . . Such numbers are not completely accurate, however, because they may not include students with invisible disabilities (such as learning disabilities or neurological or psychological impairments), nor do they include those students who refuse to be "counted" owing to the stigma that still attaches to most disabilities today.

Arlene S. Kanter, *The Relationship Between Disability Studies and the Law, in* RIGHTING EDUCATIONAL WRONGS: DISABILITY STUDIES IN LAW AND EDUCATION 1, 29-30 (Arlene S. Kanter & Beth A. Ferri eds., 2013).

It should be noted that "failure-to-accommodate" claims can be brought even after a student graduates. *See, e.g.*, Rothman v. Emory University, 123 F.3d 446 (7th Cir. 1997) (upholding dismissal of lawsuit by disabled law school graduate who claimed his poor grades—which nearly caused him to flunk out—were due to school's failure to accommodate his epilepsy).

7   *See* Dan Filler, *Historical Data: Total Number of Law Schools and Students, 1964-2012,* THE FACULTY LOUNGE, Feb. 2, 2013, *at* https://www.thefacultylounge.org/2013/02/historical-data-total-number-of-law-students-1964-2012.html.

8   *See* William E. Adams, Jr., *Annual Report of the Managing Director for the Business Meeting of the Section of Legal Education and Admis-*

sions to the Bar, AMERICAN BAR ASSOCIATION, July 2021, *at* https://www.americanbar.org/content/dam/aba/administrative/legal_education_and_admissions_to_the_bar/2021/21-legaled-annual-report-of-the-managing-director.pdf.

9   In the wake of the 2008 Great Recession, demand for legal education plummeted, forcing many law schools to drop their admission standards. *See* Joe Queenan, *Here Comes a National Plague of Dumb Lawyers*, WALL ST. J., Nov. 5, 2015, *available at* https://www.wsj.com/articles/here-comes-a-national-plague-of-dumb-lawyers-1446752404 ("Law schools are so desperate to fill classrooms that they are drastically lowering standards, according to a recent report by the nonprofit group Law School Transparency. The report says that many students may only pass the bar after numerous attempts—if at all. So America may soon suffer a plague of dumb lawyers who have trouble spelling their own names. Purry Mason. Ben Matchlock. Clarice D'Arrow. That sort of thing."). This caused the ABA to scrutinize law schools more closely. Nevertheless, between 2006 and 2019 the "growth in law schools was twice as high as [the rate of] contraction." Elizabeth G. Adelman et al., *Academic Law Library Director Status Since the Great Recession: Strengthened, Maintained, or Degraded?*, 112 LAW LIBR. J. 117, 122 (2020). As these authors further observe, "There is skepticism about the sustainability of the current business model of law schools. . . . Attaining greater student enrollment numbers, [and] thus more tuition revenue, often means accepting those with weaker credentials." *Id.* at 124 (footnote omitted). For a further discussion, see BENJAMIN H. BARTON, FIXING LAW SCHOOLS: FROM COLLAPSE TO THE TRUMP BUMP AND BEYOND (2019) (fearing, *id.* at 243-45, that legal educators have failed to learn the lessons of the Great Recession). (Barton's fears appear to be justified. In March 2022, shortly after the research for this book closed, both High Point University and Jacksonville University announced plans to open law schools. *See* Jack Crittenden, *Two New Law Schools Announced in Florida and North Carolina*, PRELAW MAG., Mar. 16, 2022,

at https://nationaljurist.com/two-new-law-schools-announced-in-florida-and-north-carolina/.)

10 Instead, such cases have been lumped together with expulsions from other types of academic programs. *See, e.g.,* Claudia G. Catalano, *Liability of Private School or Educational Institution for Breach of Contract Arising from Expulsion or Suspension of Student,* 47 A.L.R.5th 1 (1997 & 2021 Supp.); *Student's Right to Compel School Officials to Issue Degree, Diploma, or the Like,* 11 A.L.R.4th 1182 (1982 & 2021 Supp.); E.W.H., *Expulsion or Suspension from Private School or College,* 50 A.L.R. 1497 (1927 & 2021 Supp.); Roger Billings, *Plagiarism in Academia and Beyond: What is the Role of the Courts?,* 38 U.S.F. L. Rev. 391 (2004); K.B. Melear, *The Contractual Relationship Between Student and Institution: Disciplinary, Academic, and Consumer Contexts,* 30 J.C. & U.L. 175 (2003); Thomas A. Schweitzer, *"Academic Challenge" Cases: Should Judicial Review Extend to Academic Evaluations of Students?,* 41 Am. U. L. Rev. 267 (1992); Steven D. Milam & Rebecca D. Marshall, *Impact of Regents of the University of Michigan v. Ewing on Academic Dismissals from Graduate and Professional Schools,* 13 J.C. & U.L. 335 (1987); Eugene L. Kramer, *Expulsion of College and Professional Students—Rights and Remedies,* 38 Notre Dame L. Rev. 174 (1963); Scott R. Sinson, Note, *Judicial Intervention of Private University Expulsions: Traditional Remedies and a Solution Sounding in Tort,* 46 Drake L. Rev. 195 (1997); Comment, *Private Government on the Campus—Judicial Review of University Expulsions,* 72 Yale L.J. 1362 (1963); Christopher Carl Grindle, *An Analysis of Court Cases Involving Student Due Process in Dismissal from Higher Education* (unpublished Ph.D. dissertation, University of Alabama, 2009), *available at* https://ir.ua.edu/bitstream/handle/123456789/710/file_1.pdf?sequence=1&isAllowed=y.

11 In 2017, for example, Las Vegas attorney Jason J. Bach moved to withdraw as Julie Bullock's co-counsel due to "irreconcilable differences." *See* Heather Isringhausen Gvillo, *Attorney Seeks to Withdraw from Law Student's Suit Alleging Wrongful Expulsion,* Madison-St.

CLAIR REC. (Elk Grove Village, IL), May 23, 2017, *at* https://madison-record.com/stories/511118983-attorney-seeks-to-withdraw-from-law-student-s-suit-alleging-wrongful-expulsion. Several months earlier, Bach had helped Bullock institute a federal lawsuit against Southern Illinois University's law school, which had expelled her for plagiarism shortly before she was scheduled to graduate. *See* Bullock v. Board of Trs. of S. Ill. Univ. Sch. of L., Case 3:17-cv-00009-MJR-SCW (S.D. Ill.) (complaint filed Jan. 9, 2017), *available at* https://www.pacermonitor.com/view/OYXF2BQ/Bullock_v_BOARD_OF_TRUSTEES_OF_SOUTHERN__ilsdce-17-00009__0007.0.pdf. In 2018, the case was dismissed in an opinion that does not appear on either Lexis or Westlaw but can be located on PACER if one knows to look for it. *See* Bullock v. Board of Trs. of S. Ill. Univ. Sch. of L., Case 3:17-cv-00009-MJR-SCW (S.D. Ill.) (order of dismissal filed Mar. 14, 2018), *available at* https://www.pacermonitor.com/public/filings/DP65UWJA/Bullock_v_BOARD_OF_TRUSTEES_OF_SOUTHERN__ilsdce-17-00009__0056.0.pdf. Despite her expulsion, Bullock continues to list her J.D. on her *LinkedIn* page. *See Julie Bullock,* LINKEDIN, *at* https://www.linkedin.com/in/julie-bullock-34746219/ (last visited Apr. 1, 2022).

12 Of course, in some instances there is little or nothing to find. When James Naum was expelled from Willamette University's law school for leading a student protest regarding the grading of first-year exams, he filed a $450,000 lawsuit. *See Expelled Law Student is Suing Willamette,* TRI-CITY HERALD (Pasco, Kennewick, Richland, WA), Oct. 3, 1968, at 10. Diligent searching has turned up nothing further about Naum's case.

When Diana Kazolis was expelled from the University of La Verne's law school for cheating on her exams, she sought a preliminary injunction, which was denied. *See* Pat Brennan, *Court Refuses to Order Law Student Reinstated,* L.A. TIMES, Feb. 7, 1985, pt. X, at 1 (San Gabriel Valley). Although Kazolis took an appeal, no decision of any sort has been located. La Verne's opening ap-

pellate brief, however, is available at https://books.google.com/
books?id=sMdCE0PtFYQC&q=kazolis (last visited Apr. 1, 2022).

In 1991, Maurice J. Neshewat, who later changed his last name
to "Salem," was expelled from Pace University's law school for poor
grades. In 1994, his anonymously titled lawsuit was dismissed in a
"nine-page ruling filed [by] acting state Supreme Court Justice Kenneth H. Lange." *See* Bruce Golding, *'A' on Summer Law Course, 'F' in
Court,* HERALD STATESMAN (Yonkers, NY), Mar. 23, 1994, at 15A. A
copy of Justice Lange's decision has not been found. It seems likely,
however, that this case is the predecessor to Doe v. Pace Univ. Sch.
of L., 648 N.Y.S.2d 321 (App. Div. 1996). In *Doe,* the New York Appellate Division affirmed the trial court's dismissal of Doe's misrepresentation lawsuit "on the ground of res judicata." *Id.* at 321.

In 2014, a law student named Mauricio R. Celis was expelled
from the LL.M. program at Northwestern University ("NU") after
the school learned he was a felon. Although Celis sued NU, he later
voluntarily dismissed his lawsuit. *See* Dan Hinkel, *Expelled Felon
Files Suit Against NU Law,* CHI. TRIB., June 19, 2014, at 1. Several years before entering NU, Celis had been convicted in Texas of
falsely holding himself out as being a member of the Mexican bar.
See Celis v. State, 354 S.W.3d 7 (Tex. Ct. App. 2011), *aff'd,* 416 S.W.3d
419 (Tex. Ct. Crim. App. 2013).

Even when an opinion has been discovered, it sometimes has
proven impossible to categorize it. In Mewshaw v. Brooklyn L. Sch.,
383 N.Y.S.2d 648 (App. Div. 1976), for example, Joseph J. Mewshaw
sued unsuccessfully for readmission. Finding that the law school
had not abused its discretion, the appellate court affirmed the trial
court in a one-sentence opinion that sheds no light on the reason
for Mewshaw's expulsion. Mewshaw later moved to Los Angeles
and in 1993 was admitted to the California bar. *See Mewshaw, Joseph
James,* STATE BAR OF CALIFORNIA, *at* https://apps.calbar.ca.gov/at-
torney/LicenseeSearch/QuickSearch?FreeText=joseph+mewshaw&
SoundsLike=false (last visited Apr. 1, 2022).

In Goldman v. Widener Univ., Inc., Civ. A. Nos. 86-1421, 86-1497, 1986 WL 4328 (E.D. Pa. Apr. 8, 1986), Richard Ervais and Mitchell A. Goldman asked the court to enjoin their dismissal. The court responded by granting the pair a 60-day injunction without explaining why the law school was trying to expel them. On his social media profile, Ervais, who now works as a Silicon Valley executive assistant, lists his education as including "Delaware Law School 2 years toward JD." *See Richard Ervais,* LINKEDIN, *at* https://www.linkedin.com/in/richard-ervais-7769431/ (last visited Apr. 1, 2022). Goldman, on the other hand, enrolled in the Thomas M. Cooley Law School, graduated in 1992, and now practices in California. *See Mitchell Andrew Goldman #243818,* STATE BAR OF CALIFORNIA, *at* https://apps.calbar.ca.gov/attorney/Licensee/Detail/243818 (last visited Apr. 1, 2022).

In Shuman v. University of Minn. L. Sch., 451 N.W.2d 71 (Minn. Ct. App. 1990), friends and classmates Joseph Shasky and Craig Shuman were accused of plagiarism by their Contracts professor. Following protracted hearings, the law school suspended them for one year. At roughly the same time, the pair were informed that they were not eligible to return because of their poor grades. In their lawsuit (which they lost), Shasky and Shuman challenged their suspensions but not their expulsions. It is not known what happened to Shasky. Shuman, on the other hand, appears to have become a data analyst. *See Craig S.,* LINKEDIN, *at* https://www.linkedin.com/in/craig-s-90280972/ (last visited Apr. 1, 2022).

In Fetik v. New York L. Sch., No. 97 Civ. 7746 (DLC), 1998 WL 531843 (S.D.N.Y. Aug. 24, 1998), *later proceedings at* No. 97 Civ. 7746 (DLC), 1998 WL 651044 (S.D.N.Y. Sept. 23, 1998), *reconsideration denied,* No. 97 Civ. 7746 (DLC), 1999 WL 459805 (S.D.N.Y. June 29, 1999), Sheryl A. Fetik was expelled during her third year of law school. According to the court, she initially was accused "of producing and selling tapes and transcripts of law school courses." *Fetik,* 1998 WL 651044, at *2. However, as the investigation proceeded, other charges were added, including "shouting at NYLS officials." *Id.* at *3. The court ended its statement of the facts by writing: "On October 17, 1996, the ARC [Academic Responsibility Committee] published its Report. . . . The Report, which recommended that Fetik be dismissed from NYLS, was forwarded to NYLS Dean Harry [H.] Wellington. Wellington dismissed Fetik from NYLS on November 11, 1996[.]" There is no way to know from this synopsis exactly what caused Fetik to be expelled. In response to a reporter's question during her 2021 unsuccessful bid for a seat on the New York City Council, Fetik responded: "I graduated from Queens College . . . and became a licensed C.P.A. (Certified Public Accountant). I also attended law school, and am currently working on meeting the requirements to become a licensed attorney." Kayla Levy, *NYC Council District 29 Election: Sheryl Ann Fetik Seeks Seat*, Patch, June 11, 2021, *at* https://patch.com/new-york/foresthills/nyc-council-district-29-election-sheryl-ann-fetik-seeks-seat.

In Lee v. Southern Calif. Univ. for Prof'l Stud., 56 Cal. Rptr. 3d 134 (Ct. App. 2007), *later proceedings at* No. G042174, 2010 WL 5177885 (Cal. Ct. App. Dec. 22, 2010), Patricia Lee was expelled after two years of a four-year on-line J.D. program. When she was refused a refund, she filed a class action lawsuit. The courts found she could proceed but did not rule on the merits of her claim. The case later settled, with each class member receiving a future tuition voucher worth up to $1,650. *See* Sarah Mirando, *SCUPS Class Action Lawsuit Settlement*, Top Class Actions, Aug. 8, 2012, *at* https://topclassactions.com/lawsuit-settlements/lawsuit-news/scups-class-action-lawsuit-settlement/.

In Ghoshal v. Thomas M. Cooley L. Sch., No. 1:10-cv-888, 2012 WL 716143 (W.D. Mich. Feb. 17, 2012), *report and recommendation adopted*, No. 1:10-cv-888, 2012 WL 716138 (W.D. Mich. Mar. 6, 2012), Amit Ghoshal was expelled for reasons that are not identified by the court. Media reports, however, claim that Ghoshal was found guilty of "changing an exam answer during an appeal of his grade."

See Martha Neil, *Federal Court Dismisses Former Cooley Law Student's Suit Over Being Kicked Out of School,* ABA J., Mar. 10, 2012, *at* https://www.abajournal.com/news/article/federal_court_dismisses_former_cooley_law_students_suit_over_being_kicked. Ghoshal continues to list Cooley on his social media profile. *See Dr. Amit Ghoshal,* LinkedIn, *at* https://www.linkedin.com/in/dr-amit-ghoshal-781b3516/ (last visited Apr. 1, 2022).

In *In re* Extradition of Shaw, No. 14-81475-WM, 2015 WL 1622971 (S.D. Fla. Apr. 2, 2015), Shawn A. Shaw moved to represent himself and confusingly told the court "that he dropped out of [an unidentified] law school after two years because he 'flunked out' and lost his scholarship." *Id.* at *1. Regardless of whether he dropped out or flunked out, Shaw was permitted to represent himself, lost the case, and was sent to Thailand, where he was wanted for kidnapping a local businessman and demanding a $2 million ransom. *See* Paula McMahon, *Extradited to Thailand,* S. Fla. Sun-Sentinel, Dec. 10, 2016, at 3B (explaining that the victim was released unharmed and that no money exchanged hands).

Lastly, in Harrington v. Board of Sup'rs of La. St. Univ., No. 2020 CW 1012, 2020 WL 7333455 (La. Ct. App. Dec. 14, 2020), the trial court ordered Louisiana State University to either reinstate Colby S. Harrington or give him a fair hearing. The appellate court reversed on procedural grounds in a one-paragraph opinion that does not explain why Harrington was expelled.

In a case that appeared after this book's closing date, the court cryptically wrote:

> Plaintiff alleges a series of events took place on or around
> Defendant's campus involving himself, other students, faculty, and
> staff members of Defendant's law school which ultimately led to
> his dismissal from the law school. He asserts four causes of action
> against Defendant: (1) breach of contract; (2) violation of Title
> IX of the Education Amendments of 1972; (3) negligent retention
> of employees; and (4) violation of fundamental fairness and fair

dealing. Defendant does not respond to Plaintiff's alleged facts. Instead, it moves for dismissal for lack of personal jurisdiction under Federal Rule of Civil Procedure 12(b)(2).

. . . .

Plaintiff has declined to file a response brief or affidavit in support of personal jurisdiction.

. . . .

As explained above, Plaintiff has failed to make a prima facie showing of personal jurisdiction. Therefore, Defendant's motion to dismiss for lack of personal jurisdiction, Doc. 7, is **GRANTED**.

Grigoryev v. Washington & Lee Univ., Case No. 2:21-cv-1500, 2022 WL 1154758, at *1-2 (S.D. Ohio Apr. 19, 2022) (bold in original).

13 *See, e.g.,* Yu v. University of La Verne, 126 Cal. Rptr. 3d 763 (Ct. App. 2011) (although faculty prosecutor asked that law student accused of plagiarism be expelled, dean decided that grade of "0.0," suspension, and formal letter of censure constituted sufficient punishment); Viriyapanthu v. Regents of the Univ. of Calif., No. BS 071888, 2002 WL 34237152 (Cal. Super. Ct. Jan. 22, 2002), *later proceedings at* No. BS 071888, 2002 WL 34237151 (Cal. Super. Ct. Feb. 19, 2002), *aff'd,* No. B157836, 2003 WL 22120968 (Cal. Ct. App. Sept. 15, 2003), *cert. denied,* 541 U.S. 1042 (2004) (UCLA law student who admitted plagiarizing his Legal History seminar paper given "suspended dismissal" and, after serving one-semester suspension and performing community service, allowed to graduate); *In re* Zbiegien, 433 N.W.2d 871 (Minn. 1988) (although professor recommended that William Mitchell law student who committed plagiarism be expelled, associate dean decided that grade of "F," together with loss of credit and loss of tuition, amounted to adequate penalties).

In 1965, while a first-year law student at Syracuse University, future U.S. President Joe Biden worried that he was going to be expelled after it was discovered he had plagiarized five pages from a law review article. In a letter to the dean, he offered to withdraw to avoid the public disgrace of being expelled:

> I am aware that, in many instances, ignorance of the law is no excuse. Consequently, if you decide that this is such an instance and that I've broken the law, then any course of action on your part is justified. But please, I implore you, don't take my honor. If your decision is that I may not remain at Syracuse University College of Law, please allow me to resign, but don't label me a cheat.

Paul Taylor, *Biden Admits Plagiarizing in Law School*, WASH. POST, Sept. 18, 1987, *available at* https://www.washingtonpost.com/archive/politics/1987/09/18/biden-admits-plagiarizing-in-law-school/53047c90-c16d-4f3a-9317-a106be8f6102/. In the end, the faculty voted to give Biden an "F" and allowed him to repeat the course. *Id.* As a result, he was able to graduate on time and with a clean record. *Id.*

In 2011, Brad Levin (then known as Brad Carmack), a third-year law student at Brigham Young University, was threatened with expulsion after he wrote a book arguing that homosexuality and Mormonism were compatible. *See* BRAD CARMACK, HOMOSEXUALITY: A STRAIGHT BYU STUDENT'S PERSPECTIVE (2011). After graduating, Levin filed an ABA complaint against the school. *See* Paul L. Caron, *Law Student Says He was Almost Expelled from BYU for Writing Book in Favor of Gay Marriage*, TAXPROF BLOG, May 10, 2016, *at* https://taxprof.typepad.com/taxprof_blog/2016/05/law-student-says-he-was-almost-expelled-from-byu-for-writing-book-in-favor-of-gay-marriage.html. The ABA dropped its investigation after BYU agreed to "tweak" its policies. *See* Debra Cassens Weiss, *BYU Law School Says ABA Probe is Closed; Group Had Alleged Religious Discrimination*, ABA J., Aug. 19, 2016, *at* https://www.abajournal.com/news/article/byu_law_school_says_aba_probe_is_closed_group_had_alleged_religious_discrim.

Just because a law student avoids expulsion does not mean he or she is home free, for the bar examiners can relitigate the matter. *See, e.g., In re* Application of Olterman, 835 N.E.2d 370 (Ohio 2005) (although Thomas M. Cooley Law School student served one-year suspension for lying on his law school admission application, bar examiners did not err when they decided he was not fit to take the bar exam); Friedman v. Connecticut B. Examining Comm., 824 A.2d 866, 876 (Conn. App. Ct.), *certification granted,* 831 A.2d 249 (Conn. 2003), *appeal dismissed,* 853 A.2d 496 (Conn. 2004) (although dean of Quinnipiac University's law school vacated honor court's ruling that student had cheated on an exam, bar examiners "did not act arbitrarily or unreasonably or in abuse of [their] discretion or without a fair investigation of the facts . . . in concluding that the petitioner lacked good moral character."); *In re* K.S.L., 495 S.E.2d 276, 278 (Ga. 1998) (although University of Georgia exonerated student of plagiarism, bar examiners "were not bound by the law school's determination" and therefore court would not second-guess their decision finding applicant unfit for admission); Florida Bd. of B. Exam'rs re M.C.A., 650 So. 2d 34 (Fla. 1995) (reversing bar examiners' determination that Seton Hall University law student, who was found guilty of cheating, served two-semester suspension, and later was readmitted to law school and allowed to graduate, lacked good character); *In re* Application of Simmons, 584 N.E.2d 1159 (Ohio 1992) (reducing from two years to one year amount of time bar examiners had ordered University of Toledo law student to wait to take bar exam as additional penalty for misappropriating $900 from the Black Law Student Association while in law school).

14 *See, e.g., In re* Huddleston, 777 S.E.2d 438, 439 (Ga. 2015) ("While attending John Marshall Law School, [Jonathan R.] Huddleston was dismissed from the school in June 2012 for failure to meet its academic standards, but was later reinstated in August 2012, which allowed him to graduate in the spring of 2013."); Appeal of Estes, 580 P.2d 977, 977-78 (Okla. 1978) ("[William F. Estes] enrolled in

the University of Oklahoma School of Law in the fall of 1970. After completion of two semesters, in September of 1971, he was indicted by a [federal] grand jury [for] conspiracy to import marijuana into the United States from Mexico and pleaded guilty on two counts. He was sentenced to five years on each count. . . . On July 3, 1975, . . . the United States Board of Parole filed a certificate . . . unconditionally setting aside his conviction and discharging him. Applicant was readmitted to [the] law school and graduated with a Juris Doctorate in May of 1977.") (footnotes omitted).

In Baltimore Univ. v. Colton, 57 A. 14 (Md. 1904), George S. Colton was expelled for taking too long to graduate from the defendant's two-year night law school. (This school, which has no connection to the present-day University of Baltimore, became part of the University of Maryland's law school in 1913. *See Historical Sketch*, CATALOGUE AND ANNOUNCEMENT: THE LAW SCHOOL OF THE UNIVERSITY OF MARYLAND 1913-1914, at 8-9 (1913), *available at* https://www2.law.umaryland.edu/marshall/schoolarchives/documents/Catalog1913.pdf.) Colton had enrolled in 1896 but by 1901 still had not gotten his degree due to his work schedule, which made it hard for him to attend classes. In the interim, the law school's faculty resigned *en masse*. When the new faculty refused to recognize Colton as a student (even though he needed only two more courses to graduate), Colton took the school to court. *See Sues for Legal Lore*, BALT. SUN, May 21, 1902, at 6. After winning his lawsuit, Colton was able to finish his education and became a lawyer. Almost immediately, however, he ran into trouble when he was accused of selling a piece of land he did not own. *See Charges Lawyer with Deceit*, BALT. SUN, June 3, 1904, at 7 ("Daniel McKinley sued George S. Colton, a young lawyer, in the Superior Court yesterday . . . to recover $500 for alleged deceit . . . in the sale of [the] property [at] 2137 Jefferson Street."). Although McKinley won, he was awarded just one penny in damages. *See Court Proceedings*, BALT. SUN, Apr. 13, 1905, at 10.

In Littsey v. Board of Govs. of Wayne St. Univ., 310 N.W.2d 399 (Mich. Ct. App. 1981), Keith W. Littsey, a hearing-impaired student, was expelled after his first year for poor grades. When he sued, claiming that the school had illegally prohibited him from taping his classes, the trial court dismissed his complaint. After the appeals court reversed, the school agreed to readmit Littsey and give him one year's tuition as damages. *See* Brenda Gilchrist, *Handicapped Student Readmitted,* DET. FREE PRESS, Feb. 27, 1985, at 10A. In 1992, Littsey was admitted to the Michigan bar. *See Keith W. Littsey,* STATE BAR OF MICHIGAN, *at* https://sbm.reliaguide.com/lawyer/48234-MI-Keith-Littsey-27830 (last visited Apr. 1, 2022).

In Smith v. University of Det., 378 N.W.2d 511 (Mich. Ct. App. 1985), African-American students Brenda K. Sanders and Lindsey Smith were expelled for poor grades. To get back in, they sued the school for "ingrained, systematic, and studied racism." *See* Roddy Ray, *Pair Seeks Readmission: Suit Charges Bias at U of D Law School,* DET. FREE PRESS, Aug. 24, 1983, at 16B. By the time the court ruled on their claims, the suit had become a class action. *See* Brenda Gilchrist, *81 Black Students Win Trial in U-D Bias Suit,* DET. FREE PRESS, Mar. 1, 1986, at 2A. In the interim, Sanders had been readmitted and had earned her degree (Smith chose to drop out and became a substitute teacher). *Id.* Six months later, the school settled the case for $60,000. *See Racial Bias Lawsuit Against U-D Settled,* DET. FREE PRESS, Sept. 18, 1986, at 7A (reporting that Sanders and Smith each received $2,000; 22 other plaintiffs each received $545; and $40,000 went to the plaintiffs' attorneys). In 2008, Sanders became a Michigan state trial judge. After two suspensions (in 2010 and 2014), she was removed from the bench in 2015 for "mental unfitness." *See In re Sanders,* 865 N.W.2d 30 (Mich. 2015). *See also Brenda Karen Sanders,* BALLOTPEDIA, *at* https://ballotpedia.org/Brenda_Karen_Sanders (last visited Apr. 1, 2022).

In Aloia v. New York L. Sch., No. 88 Civ. 3184 (CSH), 1988 WL 80236 (S.D.N.Y. July 27, 1988), Richard J. Aloia was expelled for poor grades. Aloia blamed his sub-par performance on a medical problem ("Central Nervous System Metabolic disorder") that he had hidden from the faculty. Finding this explanation to be credible, the school advised Aloia he could return if he obtained a letter from his doctor stating that his "condition is cured or sufficiently under control." *Id.* at *4. When Aloia challenged this requirement, the court sided with the school: "The Law School's present position in respect of Aloia's status constitutes both a reasonable accommodation to his condition, and evidence supporting the inference of non-discriminatory intent." *Id.* at *9. Although it is unclear what happened next, in 1991 Aloia was admitted to the New York bar. *See Richard Aloia,* Martindale, *at* https://www.martindale.com/attorney/richard-j-aloia-544610/ (last visited Apr. 1, 2022).

In Colombini v. Members of the Bd. of Dirs. [of the Empire Coll. Sch. of Law], 232 F.3d 893 (table), No. 99-17536, 2000 WL 1125643 (9th Cir. Aug. 8, 2000), *later proceedings at* No. C9704500CR, 2001 WL 1006785 (N.D. Cal. Aug. 17, 2001), *aff'd,* 61 F. App'x 387 (9th Cir.), *cert. denied,* 540 U.S. 1000 (2003), Gene M. Colombini was expelled twice for poor grades, which he blamed on his various disabilities. Following mediation before the U.S. Department of Education's Office of Civil Rights, the two sides were able to reach a resolution. "Colombini then re-enrolled and eventually graduated from the school." *Colombini,* 2001 WL 1006785, at *2.

Lastly, in Rittenhouse v. Board of Trs. of S. Ill. Univ., 628 F. Supp. 2d 887 (S.D. Ill. 2008), Lisa D. Rittenhouse was expelled after her first year for poor grades. Claiming that she had been discriminated against because she was White and disabled, she filed a lawsuit against the school. After the court ruled that several of her claims were actionable, the school readmitted her. *See Lisa Rittenhouse,* LinkedIn, *at* https://www.linkedin.com/in/lisa-rittenhouse-12997637/ (last visited Apr. 1, 2022) (reporting that she graduated in 2012 and now works as a sole practitioner in Ogallala, Nebraska).

15 *See, e.g.,* Martin v. Helstad, 578 F. Supp. 1473 (W.D. Wis.), *aff'd,* 699
    F.2d 387 (7th Cir. 1983), *further proceedings at* Matter of Martin, 510
    N.W.2d 687, 689 (Wis. 1994) (after he was expelled from the Univer-
    sity of Wisconsin's law school for failing to reveal his federal con-
    viction for dealing in forged securities, student was admitted to, and
    graduated from, the University of California-Berkeley's law school);
    Matter of Scavone, 524 A.2d 813, 814 (N.J. 1987) (after being forced
    to withdraw from the University of Pennsylvania's law school for
    misrepresenting his race, altering his law school transcript, and ly-
    ing to potential employers about his grades, student was admitted
    to, and graduated from, St. Louis University's law school); Petition
    of Waters, 447 P.2d 661, 662-63 (Nev. 1968) (student had someone
    else take his LSAT for him—after his deception was discovered, he
    was asked to leave the University of Texas's law school; later was
    expelled from Baylor University's law school for the same reason;
    but subsequently was allowed to enroll in, and graduate from, Texas
    Southern University's law school after a brief period of study at At-
    lanta's John Marshall Law School).

Occasionally, a great deal of detective work is needed to figure
out that an expelled student later graduated from a different law
school. In Goldstein v. New York Univ., 77 N.Y.S. 80 (Sup. Ct.), *rev'd,*
78 N.Y.S. 739 (App. Div. 1902), for example, Louis Goldstein, a first-
year law student at New York University ("NYU"), sent a letter to
a female classmate (Lillian S. Newmark) asking for a date. When
Newmark complained to the dean, he questioned Goldstein about
the letter. Goldstein denied sending it and insisted that someone
was playing a practical joke on him. Summoned to a hearing before the faculty, Goldstein repeated his claim and blamed another
student named "Pfeifer." After determining (through a spelling test)
that Goldstein was lying, the faculty expelled him. *See Accused of
Flirting by Mail,* N.Y. Times, Apr. 6, 1902, at 8. Subsequently, Goldstein enrolled in New York Law School ("NYLS"), was admitted to
the New York bar in 1904, and later became a judge in Brooklyn.

See Ex-Judge Louis Goldstein Dies in Florida, WILLIAMSBURG NEWS (Brooklyn, NY), Apr. 23, 1965, at 3. Goldstein's obituary mentions his NYLS degree but says nothing about his expulsion from NYU.

In Miller v. Hamline Univ. Sch. of L., 601 F.2d 970 (8th Cir. 1979), Robert D. Miller was expelled after two years for poor grades. When he sued for reinstatement, the district court dismissed his complaint and the Eighth Circuit affirmed. Miller then went to work as a salesman for the West Publishing Company. While there, he enrolled in William Mitchell's law school and in 1989 earned his degree. *See Miller, Robert "Bob" D.,* STAR TRIB. (Minneapolis), Nov. 14, 2021, at B12 (reporting that Miller became a successful criminal defense lawyer). Ironically, by the time Miller died, Hamline and Mitchell had merged. *See* Maura Lerner, *Amid Trying Times, 2 Law Schools Decide to Become 1,* STAR TRIB. (Minneapolis), Feb. 14, 2015, at A1 ("On Friday, Hamline University and William Mitchell College of Law announced that they are merging their law schools, which have been rivals [in St. Paul] for four decades. . . . The new combined school will be called the Mitchell|Hamline School of Law, and will be located mainly on Mitchell's campus. . . .").

In Degarza v. Oklahoma City Univ., 20 P.3d 152 (Okla. Ct. Civ. App. 2000), Andre Degarza was expelled for "inappropriate behavior." *Id.* at 152 (the opinion does not indicate what Degarza did to warrant expulsion). Degarza subsequently enrolled in Texas Southern University's law school and graduated in 2004. *See Mr. Andre 'Andre' [sic] Degarza,* STATE BAR OF TEXAS, *at* https://www.texasbar.com/AM/Template.cfm?Section=Find_A_Lawyer&template=/Customsource/MemberDirectory/MemberDirectoryDetail.cfm&ContactID=297517 (last visited Apr. 1, 2022). In 2021, Degarza was suspended for one year after he admitted that "in connection [with] an adjudicatory proceeding, [he] manifested bias or prejudice based on race." *Id.*

In Forbes v. St. Thomas Univ., Inc., No. 07-22502-CIV, 2008 WL 11411866 (S.D. Fla. Aug. 28, 2008), *later proceedings at* 768 F. Supp.

2d 1222 (S.D. Fla. 2010), *and later proceedings at* No. 07-22502-CIV, 2011 WL 2118737 (S.D. Fla. May 27, 2011), *aff'd,* 456 F. App'x 809 (11th Cir. 2012), Randall V. Forbes was expelled for poor grades. After unsuccessfully suing the school for disability discrimination, she moved to New York, enrolled in New York Law School, and in 2020 became a member of the New York bar. *See Randall Vanessa Forbes,* NEW YORK STATE UNIFIED COURT SYSTEM—ATTORNEY ONLINE SERVICES—SEARCH, *at* https://iapps.courts.state.ny.us/attorneyservices/wicket/page?3 (last visited Apr. 1, 2022).

In Bradshaw v. Pennsylvania St. Univ., Civil Action No. 10-4839, 2011 WL 1288681 (E.D. Pa.), *order entered,* 2011 WL 1288695 (E.D. Pa. Apr. 5, 2011), Simone Bradshaw was expelled for poor grades. After her lawsuit against the school (for breach of contract, deprivation of property without due process, and unjust enrichment) was dismissed, she enrolled in Faulkner University's law school in Montgomery, Alabama, and graduated in 2014. *See Simone Bradshaw, Esq.,* LINKEDIN, *at* https://www.linkedin.com/in/simone-bradshaw-esq-07207692/ (last visited Apr. 1, 2022) (indicating that Bradshaw currently works in South Florida as an attorney-advisor for the U.S. Small Business Administration).

In Powers v. St. John's Univ. Sch. of L., No. 52811, 2011 WL 12883297 (N.Y. Sup. Ct. July 18, 2011), *aff'd,* 973 N.Y.S.2d 285 (App. Div. 2013), *aff'd,* 32 N.E.3d 371 (N.Y. 2015), David Powers was expelled when the school discovered he had omitted from his admission application important details regarding his convictions for dealing Ecstasy and LSD. *See* Elizabeth A. Harris, *Past Drug Charges Derail a Law Student's Education,* N.Y. TIMES, Apr. 9, 2015, at A22. After learning about the case, Bennett L. Gershman, a law professor at Pace University, succeeded in getting Powers admitted to his school. *See* Elizabeth A. Harris, *A 2nd Chance to Study Law After a 'Raw Deal,'* N.Y. TIMES, Aug. 31, 2015, at A13. Powers graduated *magna cum laude* from Pace in 2017 and currently works as an accountant, lawyer, and real estate broker in Westchester County. *See*

David Powers, LINKEDIN, *at* https://www.linkedin.com/in/david-powers/ (last visited Apr. 1, 2022).

In McLaughlin v. Florida Int'l Univ. Bd. of Trs., 533 F. Supp. 3d 1149 (S.D. Fla. 2021), *later proceedings at* Case No. 1:20-cv-22942-KMM, 2021 WL 2064895 (S.D. Fla. May 6, 2021), *aff'd,* No. 21-11453, 2022 WL 1203080 (11th Cir. Apr. 22, 2022), Christina M. McLaughlin was expelled after her first year for unsatisfactory grades. Contending that her poor performance was the result of a concerted effort by the faculty to get rid of her because she was a Donald Trump supporter, McLaughlin unsuccessfully sued the school (and numerous other parties) for violating her constitutional rights. In the meantime, McLaughlin enrolled in, and graduated from, Ave Maria Law School. *See Christy McLaughlin*, LINKEDIN, *at* https://www.linkedin.com/in/christy-mclaughlin-04b87b183/ (last visited Apr. 1, 2022) (describing herself as a "lawyer with strong Conservative principles" even though she has not passed the bar in any state).

Following the trail of Gregory Langadinos is particularly difficult, for many of his lawsuits did not result in reported opinions. Langadinos was admitted to the Southern New England School of Law ("SNESL") (the predecessor of the University of Massachusetts School of Law) in 1997 but was expelled for poor grades. In 1998, he enrolled in Touro University's law school but again was expelled for poor grades. When he then sought to return to SNESL, his application for readmission was denied. In 2002, Langadinos enrolled at the Appalachian School of Law ("ASL") and graduated from it in 2004. To date, Langadinos has not been admitted to any bar. *See Gregory Langadinos JD, MPA*, LINKEDIN, *at* https://www.linkedin.com/in/gregory-langadinos-jd-mpa-15020913b/ (last visited Apr. 1, 2022) (indicating that since 2015 he has been working as a freelance paralegal).

At different points, Langadinos filed *pro se* lawsuits against SNESL, Touro, and ASL. In these actions Langadinos collectively claimed to be a victim of disability discrimination (due to his need for accommodations under the ADA), ethnic discrimination (due to his Greek heritage), disparagement, harassment, and unlawful retaliation. Eventually, Langadinos was deemed a "vexatious litigant" and ordered not to file any new actions unless approved by a judge.

For a further discussion, see Langadinos v. Trustees of Touro Coll., 71 F. App'x 95 (2d Cir. 2003); Langadinos v. Board of Trs. of Univ. of Mass., Civil Action No. 12-11159-GAO, 2013 WL 5513796 (D. Mass. Sept. 30, 2013); Langadinos v. Appalachian Sch. of L., No. 1:05CV00039, 2005 WL 2333460 (W.D. Va. Sept. 25, 2005). *See also* Adrian Walker, *Injustice Served*, BOSTON GLOBE, Oct. 6, 2012, at B1 (explaining that in addition to SNESL, Touro, and ASL, Langadinos has sued many other parties, including his own father).

Many law schools (including my own) have adopted specific rules governing the admission of students expelled from other law schools. *See* NSU College of Law, *Disqualified Law Students, at* https://www.law.nova.edu/admission/disqualified-law-students. html (last visited Apr. 1, 2022).

16 In People *ex rel.* O'Sullivan v. New York L. Sch., 22 N.Y.S. 663 (App. Div. 1893), for example, Thomas C. O'Sullivan got into a heated argument with Dean George S. Chase just days before O'Sullivan was scheduled to graduate. As a result, the faculty voted to deny O'Sullivan his degree. *Id.* at 664-65. When O'Sullivan sued, the court sided with the school: "We see no reason why the right to discipline is not as great between the final examination and the graduation as before[.]" *Id.* at 665. The court also ruled, however, that O'Sullivan was "entitled to a certificate of attendance, and that he passed a satisfactory [competency] examination." *Id.* at 666. As a result, O'Sullivan was able to obtain his law license and later became a judge. *See O'Sullivan Dies Blessed by Pope*, N.Y. TIMES, July 29, 1913, at 1 (reporting that in 1905 O'Sullivan was elected to a seat on the New York Court of General Sessions). For a further look at the case, see *Each Says the Other Lies: Plain Talk as to Thomas C. O'Sullivan's Diploma*, N.Y. TIMES, July 31, 1892, at 8 (explaining that Chase took

offense after O'Sullivan accused him of being a bigot due to Chase's rejection of two proposed graduation speakers: a Catholic clergyman and a former U.S. Congressman of Irish heritage).

For other such cases, see Salvador v. Touro Coll. & Univ. Sys., 749 F. App'x 39 (2d Cir. 2018) (school could deny LL.M. degree to student after it belatedly discovered that his J.D. was from an online law school); Hoover v. Suffolk Univ. L. Sch., 27 F.3d 554 (table), No. 93-2074, 1994 WL 251266 (1st Cir. June 13, 1994), *cert. denied*, 519 U.S. 836 (1996) (school could deny third-year student his degree after he failed one course—although the court does not say so, it is likely that by failing the course the student lacked sufficient credits to graduate); Easley v. University of Mich. Bd. of Regents, 619 F. Supp. 418 (E.D. Mich. 1985), *later proceedings at* 627 F. Supp. 580 (E.D. Mich.), *new trial denied*, 632 F. Supp. 1539 (E.D. Mich. 1986), *remand ordered by* 853 F.2d 1351 (6th Cir. 1988), *judgment aff'd*, 906 F.2d 1143 (6th Cir. 1990), *cert. denied*, 499 U.S. 947 (1991) (school could deny degree to student who lacked sufficient credits to graduate and who also had been found guilty of plagiarism); State *ex rel.* Duffel v. Marks, 30 La. Ann. 97 (La. 1878) (refusing to recognize defendant as a law graduate of the University of Louisiana (now Tulane University)—although the university's board of administrators had voted to give the defendant his degree, such power resided exclusively in the faculty). *See also* People *ex rel.* Dorley v. Carr, 43 P. 128 (Colo. 1895) (University of Colorado law student who was denied his degree due to academic ineptitude held not qualified to take the bar exam).

In Maldonado v. Thomas M. Cooley L. Sch., 65 F. App'x. 955 (6th Cir. 2003), the Sixth Circuit affirmed the district court's dismissal of the plaintiff's lawsuit after he failed to participate in discovery:

> Jesus Mendoza Maldonado, a Texas resident proceeding pro se, appeals a district court judgment dismissing his complaint filed pursuant to 42 U.S.C. §§ 1981, 1983, 1985, and state law. . . .

Maldonado is a former student at Thomas M. Cooley Law School ("the law school"). He initiated this action in February of 1999 . . . as a result of the law school's refusal to confer a Juris Doctor degree upon him. . . .

Upon review, we conclude that the district court did not abuse its discretion in dismissing this action. . . . There is simply no doubt that Maldonado's discovery defaults have been willful and in bad faith. Further, the existence of prejudice is clear. Maldonado has completely thwarted the defendants' legitimate attempts to conduct discovery.

Id. at 955-57. In its opinion, the court does not explain the circumstances surrounding Maldonado's departure from the school. In a lengthy blog post, however, Maldonado, writing in the third person, insisted the school targeted him after he became a whistleblower:

[In] May of 1995, Jesus Mendoza started to study law at the second largest law school in the country at the Thomas M. Cooley Law School in Lansing, Michigan. Mendoza made the Dean's list and was elected President of the Hispanic Law Society for one term. During Mendoza's second year of law school, Mendoza presented to the Dean of the law school, Don Leduc, a former attorney for the US Dept. of Justice[,] concrete and specific evidence showing how the President of the law school and former Chief Justice of the Michigan Supreme Court Thomas E. Brennan and Michigan Court of Appeals [Judge] Roman S. Briggs were using the school to defraud students of their federal loans while giving away law degrees to those affiliated with government agencies. Neither [Chief Justice] Brennan, nor Judge Briggs[,] denied or engaged the evidence of fraud. Instead, Mendoza [became] the subject of pervasive harassment, illegal searches, attempts of entrapment, and attempts to run [him] over [with a vehicle]. [In] October of 1997, Mendoza was found with [an] unexplained swollen heart at the emergency room. On July 13, of 1998[,] two individuals [tried to break] into Mendoza's apartment around 3:00 am. The same day, Mendoza left the state and returned home [to] Mission, Texas. Mendoza left the law school in full compliance with the Honor Code and in good academic standing.

Jesus Mendoza, *Jesus Mendoza Targeted individual: Jesus Mendoza Update,* BLOGGER.COM, May 15, 2010, *at* http://jesusmendoza1.blogspot.com/. It has proven impossible to verify Maldonado's claim that he left the school in good standing.

17 In Mendlow v. University of Wash., No. 96 CV 5067, 1998 WL 125541 (E.D.N.Y. Mar. 16, 1998), for example, the court, in dismissing the plaintiff's complaint, wrote:

> In 1988, Carl Mendlow was a [non-law] graduate student at Yale University. He chose to leave Yale and applied to the University of Washington law school. Plaintiff applied and was accepted for admission to the University of Washington law school on or about April 15, 1989. . . .

> Following his admission, Mendlow alleges that he became the focus of his classmates' contempt. . . . Mendlow implies that this contempt was the result of his comments about women . . . and abortion . . . during class discussions. . . .

> Nonetheless, Mendlow completed his first year of law school and obtained a job as a research assistant. . . . In September of 1990, Mendlow discussed renewing his contract as a research assistant. However, on October 24, 1990, . . . Mendlow [was fired] because of complaints from Mendlow's coworkers. . . .

> In addition, Laura [J.] Buckland, a professor at the law school, complained to Dean [Robert L.] Aronson that Mendlow was sexually harassing her. . . . Dean Aronson had previously received other complaints about Mendlow's behavior. . . . As a result, Dean Aronson became concerned about Mendlow's mental stability. Dean Aronson asked Mendlow to get assurances that he would

remain safe to attend the law school. . . . Mendlow was unable to get such an assurance. Consequently, Dean Aronson asked Mendlow to obtain a psychological evaluation from Dr. Arifulla Khan and Dr. Murray [A.] Raskind at the University's medical center. . . . The evaluation indicated that Mendlow posed a danger to others. . . . Professor Buckland ultimately obtained a temporary restraining order against Mendlow . . . because he was sexually harassing her. . . . The effect of the restraining order was to bar Mendlow from the law school grounds. . . .

On October 13, 1990, early in Mendlow's second year of law school, the University police served Mendlow notice that he had been suspended from the school of law. . . . He was also notified that Professor Buckland had obtained a restraining order against him. . . . On October 26, 1990, . . . the King County Superior Court extended the restraining order for one year. The next day, Mendlow moved to Pittsburgh and did not return to the University of Washington. . . .

Id. at *1.

In Truell v. Regent Univ. Sch. of L., Civil Action No. 2:04cv716, 2005 WL 1926645 (E.D. Va. Aug. 5, 2005), *later proceedings at* Civil Action No. 2:04cv716, 2006 WL 2076769 (E.D. Va. July 21, 2006), Liane J. Truell, a first-year student, was suspended after the school discovered she had written three course evaluations in which she falsely accused her professors of racial discrimination and sexual harassment. *See Truell,* 2006 WL 2076769, at *1-2. Four months later, having refused the school's request that she undergo a psychiatric evaluation, Truell was informed "that she would be expelled from school if she did not withdraw. Plaintiff agreed to withdraw. . . ." *Id.* at *2. Truell's subsequent breach of contract lawsuit against the school was dismissed for failure to respond to discovery requests and failure to state a claim. *Id.* at *7. By this time, Truell had left Virginia and moved to Georgia. *Id.* at *1.

In Valente v. University of Dayton, 689 F. Supp. 2d 910 (S.D. Ohio 2010), *motion to amend or alter judgment denied*, Case No. 3:08-cv-225, 2010 WL 11538408 (S.D. Ohio Feb. 22, 2010), *aff'd*, 438 F. App'x 381 (6th Cir. 2011), John T. Valente was suspended "for at least three semesters" for cheating on his Criminal Law exam. Rather than try to resume his studies, Valente opened EEO Advocates, a Washington, D.C. "private legal service firm providing non-attorney representation to victims of employment discrimination claims." *See John Valente*, LINKEDIN, *at* https://www.linkedin.com/in/john-valente-a669484/ (last visited Apr. 1, 2022) (listing Valente as the company's "Senior Legal Representative"). *See also* Valente v. Porter, Wright, Morris & Arthur, L.L.P., No. 95499, 2010 WL 5239186 (Ohio Ct. App. Dec. 16, 2010) (affirming dismissal of Valente's breach-of-confidentiality claim against the university's lawyers).

In Liu v. Northwestern Univ., 578 F. Supp. 3d 839 (N.D. Ill. 2015), Annie Liu took a medical leave of absence after her second year of law school. When she tried to return, the school refused to let her back in until she fulfilled certain "academic conditions." These conditions had been imposed after Liu had failed to meet the deadline for turning in three papers. Liu explained that she had experienced computer problems, but when the school sought to examine her computer she objected. With the school continuing to insist on seeing her computer, Liu filed a disability discrimination lawsuit. Although the court dismissed most of her complaint, it held that she had made out a colorable complaint for breach of contract due to the school's failure to follow the procedures set out in its handbook. *See id.* at 848. For unknown reasons, Liu did not pursue her lawsuit and now works as a freelance executive assistant in Los Angeles. *See Annie Liu*, LINKEDIN, *at* https://www.linkedin.com/in/liuchenannie/.

In Odemena v. Devlin, Civil Action No. 14-cv-12591-ADB, 2015 WL 13376541 (D. Mass. June 24, 2015), Martin Odemena was suspended from the Massachusetts School of Law ("MSL") after his first year for poor grades. He also was issued a "not-in-good-standing" letter. When Odemena tried to enroll at other law schools, he was unsuccessful. Contending that MSL had treated him unfairly "and ended his pursuit of a legal career," he sued the school for breach of contract and violation of the Massachusetts Consumer Protection Act. *Id.* at *1. The district court dismissed Odemena's lawsuit for failure to state a claim. *Id.* at *5.

In Shinabargar v. Board of Trs. of the Univ. of the D.C., 164 F. Supp. 3d 1 (D.D.C. 2016), a disabled law student named Nancy A. Shinabargar was suspended for inappropriate behavior. Believing she had been singled out because of her disability, as well as the numerous reports she had written accusing the faculty and her classmates of plagiarism, she filed a retaliation lawsuit against the school, which was dismissed as factually baseless. *Id.* at 33. By this time, Shinabargar had left D.C. and moved to Reno, Nevada. *Id.* at 8.

In Karimi v. Golden Gate Sch. of L., Case No. 17-cv-05702-JCS, 2018 WL 1911804 (N.D. Cal. Apr. 23, 2018), *later proceedings at* 361 F. Supp. 3d 956 (N.D. Cal. 2019), *aff'd,* 796 F. App'x 462 (9th Cir. 2020), Morteza B.R. Karimi, a first-year student, was placed on "indefinite interim suspension" for "behavioral issues." *Id.* at 961-62. While unsuccessfully suing the school for numerous alleged breaches, Karimi enrolled in Texas Southern University's law school, graduated in 2021, and became a member of the Texas bar. *See* Texas Southern University, *2021 Spring Commencement,* at 11, *available at* http://www.tsu.edu/commencement/pdf/2021-spring-commencement-2.pdf; State Bar of Texas, *Morteza Benjamin 'Ben' Karimi, at* https://www.texasbar.com/AM/Template.cfm?Section=Find_A_Lawyer&template=/Customsource/MemberDirectory/MemberDirectoryDetail.cfm&ContactID=367972 (last visited Apr. 1, 2022).

In Mateo v. University Sys. of N.H., Civil Action No. 18-11953-FDS, 2019 WL 199890 (D. Mass. Jan. 14, 2019), Joel Mateo withdrew "while under investigation for violating the school's code of conduct. Two years after withdrawing, Mateo was unable to obtain transfer admission to other law schools, apparently in part due to the unresolved conduct issue. He was also denied readmission to UNH Law." *Id.* at *1. When he sued the school, the court, after dismissing his defamation claim, ordered his other claims (for denial of due process and intentional infliction of emotional distress) transferred to the District of New Hampshire. *Id.* at *9. Once there, the school moved for, and was granted, summary judgment. *See* Mateo v. University Sys. of N.H., Case No. 19-cv-70-PB, 2020 WL 4059884 (D.N.H. July 20, 2020), *aff'd*, No. 20-1819, 2021 WL 7159934 (1st Cir. Aug. 27, 2021). According to his social media profile, Mateo remains eager to become a lawyer. *See Joel Mateo,* LinkedIn, *at* https://www.linkedin.com/in/joel-mateo-29889a48/ (last visited Apr. 1, 2022) (describing himself as a "Young professional seeking legal experience[.]").

Lastly, in Elansari v. United States, 823 F. App'x. 107 (3d Cir. 2020), Amro A. Elansari was suspended from Pennsylvania State University—Dickinson Law School for two years for making unwanted advances towards a female classmate. *Id.* at 112. Because Elansari refused to abide by the terms of his suspension, Dickinson obtained a state court injunction barring him from entering the law school. *Id.* Believing his constitutional rights had been violated, Elansari sued Dickinson. *Id.* at 109. The district court granted Dickinson's motion for summary judgment. *Id.* at 111-12. In its affirmance, the Third Circuit explained that Dickinson's "decision to suspend [Elansari] was not 'beyond the pale of reasoned academic decision-making' or otherwise the result of an arbitrary and deliberate abuse of authority." *Id.* at 112. According to his *LinkedIn* page, Elansari currently is the chief executive officer of a Philadelphia-area business called "Pennsylvania Writing Services." *See Amro Elansari,* LinkedIn, *at* https://www.linkedin.com/in/amro-elansari-8ab877130/ (last visited Apr. 1, 2022).

18 *See, e.g.,* Los v. Wardell, 771 F. Supp. 266 (C.D. Ill. 1991) (suit by University of Illinois law student against various law enforcement officials who helped enforce his expulsion); *In re* Kluksdahl, 62 So. 3d

189 (La. Ct. App. 2011) (suit by Loyola University New Orleans law student against various mental health professionals who provided information that led to his expulsion); *In re* McGrath, 915 N.Y.S.2d 107 (App. Div. 2010) (bar complaint by Cornell University law student against lawyer who allegedly mishandled her expulsion appeal). *See also* Rollins v. Wyrick, 574 F.2d 420 (8th Cir.), *cert. denied,* 439 U.S. 868 (1978) (University of Missouri student who was expelled from law school after it was discovered he was selling marijuana was not prejudiced in his subsequent criminal trial by the publicity generated by his expulsion).

   In 2003, Thomas M. Cooley Law School expelled (for the second time) Jean D. Baptichon for poor grades. Since then, Baptichon has sued the U.S. Department of Education, the State of Michigan, the school, the school's lawyer, a student loan processing company, and his own lawyer. *See* Baptichon v. United States Dep't of Educ., 20-CV-2400 (PKC) (LB), 2020 WL 6565126 (E.D.N.Y. Nov. 20, 2020); Baptichon v. Michigan, No. 1:18-cv-550, 2018 WL 3360953 (W.D. Mich. July 9, 2018); Baptichon v. Thomas M. Cooley L. Sch., No. 1:09-cv-562, 2009 WL 5214911 (W.D. Mich. Dec. 28, 2009). Baptichon also has filed many other baseless lawsuits, including one in which he demanded $20 billion from the federal government for reneging on its alleged promise to award him a "Presidential Medal of Merit." *See* Baptichon v. United States, 342 F. App'x 617 (Fed. Cir. 2009) (explaining, *id.* at 618, that no such medal exists).

19 In Miranda v. Miranda, No. FA000504376S, 2001 WL 1204284 (Conn. Super. Ct. Apr. 16, 2001), for example, the plaintiff sued her daughter for the right to visit her granddaughter. In describing the parties' relationship, the court wrote, without elaboration: "While attending [an unidentified] law school (prior to her dismissal), [the daughter] paid no rent to her mother." *Id.* at *1.

   In Hines v. Irvington Counseling Ctr., 933 F. Supp. 382 (D.N.J. 1996), a former law student sued various parties, accusing them of wrongfully withholding his disability benefits. According to the court, the plaintiff's problems began following an incident with his dean, which led to the plaintiff's hospitalization for psychiatric problems and subsequent expulsion from law school. *Id.* at 386. The court does not provide the name of either the law school or the dean.

In C.B.D. v. W.E.B., 298 N.W.2d 493 (N.D. 1980), a messy paternity case, the court noted that "Walter [the putative father] flunked out of [the University of North Dakota's] law school and moved back to Fargo in January of 1977 where he began working as a realtor."). *Id.* at 495.

See also Ayyad v. Gonzales, Civil Action No. 05-cv-02342-WYD-MJW, 2008 WL 203420, at *8 (D. Colo. Jan. 17, 2008), *vacated on other grounds,* Civil Action Nos. 05-cv-02342-WYD-MJW, 05-cv-02653, 2008 WL 2955964 (D. Colo. July 31, 2008) (noting that clinical students at the University of Denver can get "kicked out of law school" if they violate a prison's inmate visitation rules); Pearson v. Townsend, 362 F. Supp. 207, 210 n.3 (D.S.C. 1973) ("It was represented to the court at the hearing of this matter that both Inmate Representatives had completed two years of law school at the time they represented plaintiffs herein before the Adjustment Committee. While that representation appears to be true as to Hood, counsel for defendants subsequently informed the court that the other Inmate Representative had completed only one year of law school as of the summer of 1972, was not readmitted in the Autumn 1972 Term due to a deficient grade point average, but is eligible for readmission in September 1973, as a first-year student.").

In Williams v. State, 669 N.E.2d 1372 (Ind. 1996), *cert. denied,* 520 U.S. 1232 (1997), the Indiana Supreme Court held that the trial court did not err when it refused to excuse a murder case juror who had misunderstood a question during *voir dire.* According to the Court, the hypothetical would have baffled even a law student:

> The defense indicated that it sought to strike prospective juror
> Bobalik, a white female, because she failed to understand the

presumption of innocence. During voir dire, defense counsel had asked all the members of the panel who believed that the defendant was not guilty at that point to raise their hands. Bobalik was apparently the only juror who did not raise his or her hand. The trial court rejected this reason, commenting that counsel had asked "a trick question," the kind "that get students flunked out of law school." Because counsel did "not have a record showing that Bobalik [could] not give the defendant the presumption of innocence," the trial court refused to excuse Bobalik. . . .

Id. at 1380.

20 As has been explained elsewhere, "Some law schools offer programs where admission is contingent upon the successful completion of a pre-enrollment program. These programs are available for students with low numerical qualifications and are usually offered in the summer before first-year classes begin." Law School Admission Council, *Conditional Admission Programs, at* https://www.lsac.org/discover-law/diversity-law-school/raciallyethnically-diverse-applicants/conditional-admission (last visited Apr. 1, 2022) (indicating that 13 law schools currently have such programs). For a case in which two conditional students unsuccessfully sued after they flunked out, see McAlpin v. Burnett, 185 F. Supp. 2d 730, 732 (W.D. Ky. 2001) ("Plaintiffs, Timothy J. McAlpin and Leslie Dean bring this action against Defendants, Donald L. Burnett, former Dean and a professor at the University of Louisville School of Law . . . and Professor R. Thomas Blackburn for breach of contract, violation of 42 U.S.C. § 1983, and various other state law torts. These claims arise from the Law School's decision to deny Plaintiffs admission after each flunked an exam in the Law School's 'Admission by Performance Program.'") (footnote omitted).

21 In Hash v. University of Ky., 138 S.W.3d 123 (Ky. Ct. App. 2004), for example, Marcus T. Hash, with the encouragement of the faculty, withdrew from his first year of law school because of depression. When he sought to return, he was told he had missed the dead-

line. He therefore submitted a new application, which was rejected. When his request for reconsideration was denied, he sued the
school for disability discrimination. *Id.* at 124-25. In finding that the
trial court correctly granted the school's motion for summary judgment, the Kentucky Court of Appeals wrote:

> Here, the record indicates that the University's academic stan-
> dards encompass successful time management, fulfilling scheduled
> deadlines, engagement in Socratic classroom discussions and
> successful performance on intense examinations, which are all
> an integral part of completing the legal education and preparing
> for success as a practicing attorney. As such, the qualification of
> a disabled individual "turns not only on whether he or she meets
> its reasonable standards but whether the individual, where a few .
> . . must be chosen out of thousands of applicants, is as well quali-
> fied despite the handicap as others accepted for one of the limited
> number of openings." [*Doe v. New York University,* 666 F.2d 761, 776
> (2d Cir. 1981).] Accordingly, the University concluded, in its profes-
> sional judgment, and based on the reasonable academic standards
> in place that appellant was not a qualified applicant in spite of his
> depression.
>
> Therefore, we find that appellant failed to prove his prima facie
> case, as he was not an "otherwise qualified handicapped person"
> apart from his disability.

Id. at 129.

22 In its role as the national accreditor of law schools, the ABA requires (in Standard 308: "Academic Standards") that each law school
have a process for disciplining, and when necessary, expelling law
students. *See* ABA LAW SCHOOL STANDARDS, *supra* note 3 of this
chapter, at 21.

A handful of law schools (some of which are mentioned in this
book) exist that are not ABA-approved. California has the largest
number of such law schools. *See* Law School Admission Council,

Non-ABA-Approved Law Schools, at https://www.lsac.org/choosing-law-school/find-law-school/non-aba-approved-law-schools (last visited Apr. 1, 2022) (list of 32 U.S.-based non-ABA-approved law schools, of which 28 are in California). California's rules for such law schools (which can be either "accredited" or "unaccredited") include provisions that are substantially identical to Standard 308. *See* STATE BAR OF CALIFORNIA, GUIDELINES FOR ACCREDITED LAW SCHOOL RULES (effective Apr. 23, 2021) (under Rules 2.6 and 2.7), *available at* https://www.calbar.ca.gov/Portals/0/documents/admissions/AccreditedLawSchoolGuidelines.pdf, and [CALIFORNIA] COMMITTEE OF BAR EXAMINERS, GUIDELINES FOR UNACCREDITED LAW SCHOOL RULES (effective Jan. 1, 2008; last amended Jan. 1, 2021) (under Rule 5.19), *available at* https://www.calbar.ca.gov/Portals/0/documents/admissions/GuidelinesforUnaccreditedLawSchoolRules.pdf.

23 *See, e.g.,* Aishaah R. Reed, *Opportunities for Virginia Law Schools to Implement Restorative Justice Approaches in the Honor Code System,* 23 RICH. PUB. INT. L. REV. 381 (2020); Lori A. Roberts & Monica M. Todd, *Let's Be Honest About Law School Cheating: A Low-Tech Solution for A High-Tech Problem,* 52 AKRON L. REV. 1155 (2018); Erin Lain, *Experiences of Academically Dismissed Black and Latino Law Students: Stereotype Threat, Fight or Flight Coping Mechanisms, Isolation and Feelings of Systemic Betrayal,* 45 J.L. & EDUC. 279 (2016); Nicola A. Boothe-Perry, *Enforcement of Law Schools' Non-Academic Honor Codes: A Necessary Step Towards Professionalism?,* 89 NEB. L. REV. 634 (2011); Lynn Daggett, *Doing the Right Thing: Disability Discrimination and Readmission of Academically Dismissed Law Students,* 32 J.C. & U.L. 505 (2006); Steven K. Berenson, *What Should Law School Student Conduct Codes Do?,* 38 AKRON L. REV. 803 (2005); Sarah Ann Bassler, *Public Access to Law School Honor Code Proceedings,* 15 NOTRE DAME J.L. ETHICS & PUB. POL'Y 207 (2001); Penn Lerblance, *Legal and Educational Aspects of Student Dismissals: A View from the Law School,* 33 Sw L.J. 605 (1979); Meredith C. Manuel, Note, *Snitches Get Stitches: Ditching the Toleration Clause in Law*

School Honor Codes, 33 GEO. J. LEGAL ETHICS 703 (2020); Kimberly C. Carlos, Comment, *The Future of Law School Honor Codes: Guidelines for Creating and Implementing Effective Honor Codes,* 65 UMKC L. REV. 937 (1997). *See also* Terri LeClercq, *Failure to Teach: Due Process and Law School Plagiarism,* 49 J. LEGAL EDUC. 236 (1999).

24 As a result, "apprentice" disputes are not included. *See, e.g.,* Wilson v. Whitacre, 2 Ohio C.D. 392 (1889) (reversing, on procedural grounds, a jury verdict finding that Wallace D. Wilson had libeled his apprentice, William H. Whitacre, by sending a letter to the Ohio Supreme Court claiming that Whitacre was dishonest and unfit to be a lawyer). *See also William Whitacre, Father of Xenian, Removed by Death,* Gaz. (Xenia, OH), Oct. 17, 1936, at 3 (obituary explaining that Whitacre ended up spending his life selling insurance).

Until the early 20th century, the apprentice system (also known as "reading the law") was the method most Americans used to become lawyers. *See* Dorothy E. Finnegan, *Raising and Leveling the Bar: Standards, Access, and the YMCA Evening Law Schools, 1890-1940,* 55 J. LEGAL EDUC. 208, 209 (2005) ("In 1870, only one-fourth of those admitted to the bar were law school graduates [but by] 1910 two-thirds were."); Brian J. Moline, *Early American Legal Education,* 42 WASHBURN L.J. 775, 801 (2004) ("As of 1900, more than half of American lawyers had not attended law school or even college."). Today, only a few states still authorize law reading:

> Besides California, the states that allow aspiring lawyers to take the
> bar exam after reading the law, without law school, are Virginia,
> Vermont and Washington. In three other states—New York, Maine
> and Wyoming—aspiring lawyers can study in a law office, com-
> bined with some period of time in law school.

Debra Cassens Weiss, *Students Try to Avoid Law School Costs with 'Reading Law' Path to Law License,* ABA J., July 30, 2014, *at* https://www.abajournal.com/news/article/want_to_avoid_the_costs_of_law_school_these_students_try_reading_law_path_t. Accordingly, some students who are expelled from law school manage to qualify for the bar by becoming law readers.

25 "In 1505, a number of [the members of] Lincoln's Inn were expelled for watching with swords and clubs and having strife with Grey's Inn." Frances Anne Keay, *Student Days at the Inns of Court,* 75 U. Pa. L. Rev. 50, 56 (1926). This incident appears to be the first documented example of students being expelled from what we now would recognize as a law school. For a further discussion, see David Pal-freyman, London's Inns of Court: History, Law, Customs and Modern Purpose 20-22 (2011) (explaining that the Inns of Court were founded beginning in c. 1320 to educate future barristers).

In 1884, five law students at Laval University in Quebec were expelled when they refused to follow the school's dress code, which required academic gowns to be worn to class. *See The Laval Students: The Rector Gives Way, But the Students Refuse to be Comforted,* Montreal Daily Star, Nov. 15, 1884, at 8.

In the 2018 "Bracton Law Society Scandal," an undisclosed number of law students at the University of Exeter were expelled after it was discovered they had shared racist messages during private Whatsapp group chats. *See Exeter University Law Students Expelled Over Racist WhatsApp Messages,* The Week, May 2, 2018, *at* https://www.theweek.co.uk/93321/exeter-university-law-students-expelled-over-racist-whatsapp-messages.

The most famous foreign figure to be expelled from law school is Vladimir Lenin:

> Lenin's revolutionary career began immediately after the execution of his brother. As soon as he entered the Law School of the Kazan [Imperial] University, in 1887 [when he was 17], Lenin affiliated himself with a secret revolutionary circle. . . .

> In December, 1887, he was expelled from the University for participating in student riots, was forbidden to live in Kazan, and put under the secret surveillance of the police.

In July, 1888, [Lenin's] mother asked that her son Vladimir be readmitted into the University in September [1888]. . . . [Lenin] himself asked for permission to go abroad to complete his education in one of the foreign universities. Both applications were denied. . . .

In [1889 Lenin] asked to be allowed to [take] the examinations for admission to the bar. . . .

Lenin . . . passed successfully the examinations in the Law School of the St. Petersburg University in 1891. . . .

In June [1892 Lenin] asked to be admitted to the bar in Samara. In July, 1892, the president of the Samara District Court was informed that there was no obstacle to [Lenin's] admission . . . to [the] practice law.

ISAAC DON LEVINE, THE MAN LENIN 7-9 (1924) (paragraphing and punctuation slightly altered for improved readability).

26 *See, e.g.*, Zhang v. University of W. Ont., [2010] 328 D.L.R. (4th) 289 (Can. Ont. Ct. App.) (upholding expulsion of law student who posted threatening images on Facebook). *See also Nigerian Law School Shuns Court Order, Prevents Kayode Bello from Registering for Final Examination,* SAHARA REPORTERS, Aug. 11, 2017, *at* http://saharareporters. com/2017/08/11/nigerian-law-school-shuns-court-order-prevents- kayode-bello-registering-final-examination (describing Olusegun Kayode Bello's expulsion from, and subsequent lawsuit against, the Nigerian Law School—depending on whose account one believes, Bello either was expelled for drawing attention to the school's inadequate facilities or because he repeatedly engaged in disruptive behavior). In 2020, Bello wrote a book about his unsuccessful effort to be readmitted. *See* KAYODE BELLO, KAY BELLO'S REJOINDERS + ACTIVISM (2020), *available at* https://www.amazon.com/BELLOS- REJOINDERS-ACTIVISM-KAYODE-BELLO/dp/B0851M28F4.

Chapter 2

PRE-1970 EXPULSION CASES

The earliest reported law school expulsion case I have found is *Koblitz v. Western Reserve University.*[1] On September 10, 1900, Harry Koblitz was expelled for insubordination and poor grades.[2] Although a state court granted Koblitz's request for an injunction,[3] on appeal the Ohio Circuit Court found his complaint baseless:

> The testimony before us tends to show, and, we think, does fairly show, that the plaintiff's scholarship in the school has been poor and that, while a student during the year that he attended the law school, he was twice arrested on criminal charges; that he carried a revolver and threatened to inflict violence upon a fellow student; he indulged in abusive language and disorderly conduct towards fellow-students in and out of the school building; he was untruthful. When he was notified by the faculty to appear before them by reason of some of these offenses, . . . he said that he did not know whether he would go or not, that if they undertook to discipline him, they would find they had a lawsuit on their hands, and the evidence shows that he was a disturbing element in the school and a very undesirable student. . . .
>
> It seems to us that such conduct from a young man who has a fair mind and an honest purpose, is impossible. And we believe that the authorities were entirely right in refusing him admittance upon the second year.[4]

In *Gleason v. University of Minnesota,*[5] John L. Gleason was expelled after completing two years of law school.[6] According to a resolution passed by the faculty, Gleason "was dropped at the end of the year on account of deficiency in his work; and [for] certain insubordinate acts toward the faculty of the University of Minnesota and [for] inciting younger students to [commit] insubordinate acts towards said faculty."[7]

When Gleason sued for reinstatement, the school filed a demurrer.[8] This turned out to be a mistake, for the trial court overruled it.[9] On appeal, the Minnesota Supreme Court affirmed its decision to do so:

> We do not feel at liberty to construe the resolution in this instance to mean that registration was refused upon the ground that the relator had not, in good faith, applied himself to his studies. 'Deficiency in his work' does not necessarily imply persistent inattention and failure to take advantage of his opportunities, and the fact that he was 'charged' with insubordination does not warrant the inference that he was guilty, or that he had proved himself in all respects unworthy to be retained as a student. We are of [the] opinion, therefore, that the petition states a prima facie case for registration, and that the Regents should show cause, as directed by the court below.[10]

In *People ex rel. Goldenkoff v. Albany Law School*,[11] Jacob M. Goldenkoff, a senior law student, was expelled during the first Red Scare after five of his classmates accused him of being a Socialist.[12] Although Goldenkoff denied the charge and insisted "he was 100 per cent. American, and an enrolled Republican,"[13] the school decided that Goldenkoff was unfit to remain a law student.[14]

Following his dismissal, Goldenkoff sued and was ordered readmitted by the trial court.[15] In reversing this decision, the New York Appellate Division wrote:

> In this case it is not in dispute that on many occasions the petitioner gave expression to views which were unpatriotic, revolutionary, and anarchistic; that these expressions were known to the faculty of the Albany Law School; that they constituted in part the grounds of their

decision in favor of his expulsion. Clearly, therefore, the faculty acted within the scope of its jurisdiction, and exercised its discretion in a matter involving discretion, to such purpose that no review thereof may be made by a court.[16]

Lastly, in *White v. Portia Law School*,[17] Jama A. White was expelled after it was discovered she was using her law school training to avoid her debts and pursue frivolous litigation and, to make matters worse, was bragging about her exploits to her classmates.[18] When White sued for reinstatement (and $20,000 in damages), the trial court referred the case to a master, who found that the school had acted properly.[19] On appeal, the Massachusetts Supreme Judicial Court affirmed:

> The facts found warranted the master in finding that the continued presence of the plaintiff at the Portia Law School would be subversive of the discipline of the school, would tend to cast a shadow upon the reputation of the institution, and consequently would affect its power to graduate pupils imbued with good principles and impressed with high ideals of the profession of the law.[20]

After *White*, no further pre-1970 expulsion decisions involving law students have been located. However, there are two cases—one decided in 1964 and the other in 1969—in which two different night law students who were expelled for poor grades unsuccessfully sought to deduct the cost of their legal education from their federal taxes.[21] Coincidentally, both students attended Chicago's John Marshall Law School.

1   11 Ohio C.D. 515 (1901). In 1967, Western Reserve University merged with the Case Institute of Technology to form Case Western Reserve University. *See Case and WRU Ratify Merger,* AKRON BEACON J., June 2, 1967, at A27.

2   *See Koblitz,* 11 Ohio C.D. at 516-17.

3   *See Enjoins College Faculty,* MUSCATINE WKLY. NEWS-TRIB. (IA), Oct. 26, 1900, at 16 ("The best legal talent was employed by both sides and the case was hotly contested [in the Court of Common Pleas]. Judge [William B.] Neff's ruling indicates that the college faculties are not supreme in their rulings.").

4   *Koblitz,* 11 Ohio C.D. at 525.

     Despite his expulsion, Koblitz became a lawyer in 1903. *See* J.B. MARTINDALE, MARTINDALE'S AMERICAN LAW DIRECTORY 1053 (1904) (identifying Koblitz as a sole practitioner). (As explained *supra* note 24 of Chapter 1, having a law degree was not yet a prerequisite for bar admission.) Koblitz suffered from severe mental problems, however, and died in 1914. *See Ohio Lawyer is Believed Insane,* DET. FREE PRESS, Feb. 17, 1914, at 3 (describing Koblitz's arrest during a manic episode); *Harry Kobitz,* FIND A GRAVE, *at* https://www.findagrave.com/memorial/128536865/harry-koblitz (last visited Apr. 1, 2022) (indicating that Koblitz passed away at the age of 35 — suicide seems likely).

5   116 N.W. 650 (Minn. 1908).

6   *Id.* at 650.

7   *Id.* at 652.

8   *Id.* at 650.

9   *Id.*

10 *Id.* at 652. Deciding he had been vindicated, Gleason voluntarily dismissed his complaint. *See John L. Gleason Drops Case Against University*, Minneapolis Trib., Sept. 22, 1908, at 7. Gleason later opened a barber shop in Minneapolis. *See U.S., World War I Draft Registration Cards, 1917-1918 for John Leo Gleason, available at* https://www.ancestry.com/discoveryui-content/view/29974655:6482.

For a further look at *Gleason*, see Scott M. Gelber, Courtrooms and Classrooms: A Legal History of College Access, 1860-1960, at 94-95 (2016). As this source explains:

> *Gleason* originated as a dispute between students and faculty over control of the university's athletics program. Whereas students had initially managed sports teams, a national movement to reform college football prompted the University of Minnesota and most other institutions to transfer control to administrators and faculty. Led by John L. Gleason, a popular law student and president of a defunct athletics board, students argued that extracurricular activities should remain outside the sphere of faculty power. Gleason organized rallies and participated in a debate with a professor who chaired a new faculty-led athletics committee. According to a reporter, Gleason relished the role of provocateur and "flaunted the flag of defiance in the face of the faculty."

Id. at 94.

11 191 N.Y.S. 349 (App. Div. 1921).

12 *Goldenkoff*, 191 N.Y.S. at 350-51 (explaining that Goldenkoff was expelled on April 27, 1920). For a detailed look at the first Red Scare, see Robert K. Murray, Red Scare: A Study in National Hysteria, 1919-1920 (1955). As Murray explains, "The taproots of [the Great Red Scare] lay embedded in the various events growing out of the Bolshevik Revolution of November 1917." *Id.* at 15.

13 *Goldenkoff*, 191 N.Y.S. at 351.

14 *Id.* at 352 (quoting Dean J. Newton Fiero as saying: "I find that your offensive propaganda in favor of Socialism and your views make you an undesirable, and further connection with this school is denied you. You may no longer enjoy the benefits of the institution.").

15 *Id.* at 350. Goldenkoff's victory was met with indignation by his classmates, who twice walked out in protest. *See Quit Classes in Protest: Albany Law Students Refuse to Sit with Alleged Socialist,* N.Y. Times, May 13, 1920, at 3; *Students Strike Again: Walk Out of Albany Law School When Expelled Pupil Returns,* N.Y. Times, May 19, 1920, at 5.

16 *Goldenkoff,* 191 N.Y.S. at 353-54.

Despite his expulsion, Goldenkoff was admitted to the New York bar in 1926. *See* 2 Martindale-Hubbell Law Directory 2239 (1963) (listing Goldenkoff's admission date). By the time he reached middle age, Goldenkoff had become a capitalist and in 1948 was arrested for profiteering. *See* Norma Abrams & Jim Davis, *DA Vows End of Gouging—Arrests 10,* Daily News (NY), Nov. 17, 1948, at 3 ("Jacob N. [sic] Goldenkoff, 48, of 574 West End Ave., also an attorney. Described as an agent for an apartment house at 352 Central Park West, he is charged with taking from three persons a total of $765. He was arrested by detectives after he purportedly accepted $500 in marked money from a tenant for a $57.50-a-month apartment.").

17 174 N.E. 187 (Mass. 1931), *cert. denied,* 288 U.S. 611 (1933).

While the Massachusetts Supreme Judicial Court cites White's name as "James A. White," *see id.* at 187, and the U.S. Supreme Court uses "Jamea A. White," *see id.* at 611, her actual name was "Jama A. White." *See, e.g., Woman Sues Portia Law School, Asking $20,000,* Boston Globe, Apr. 23, 1929, at 8 ("Mrs. Jama A. White of Boston, who claims to have been expelled from Portia Law School in 1926, 'without a hearing,' filed yesterday in Supreme Judicial Court, a petition for a writ of mandamus. . . ."). *See also Deaths,* BOSTON SUN. GLOBE, July 19, 1981, at 59 (under "White").

During White's attendance (1923-26), Portia was an all-female law school (the only one in the country). In 1938, however, it became co-ed. In 1969, it changed its name to the "New England School of Law." Since 2008, it has been known as "New England Law Boston." *See* New England Law Boston, *Our History, at* https://www.nesl.edu/about/history (last visited Apr. 1, 2022). As this source further explains:

> New England Law | Boston began in 1908 as Portia Law School, which offered a legal education exclusively to women at a time when most other institutions would not accept them at all. The early Portia Law School students were primarily from working-class and immigrant families and many had only a high school education, since the state did not require a college degree to study law. For decades, most of the women who passed the Massachusetts bar examination were Portia graduates.

Id.

18 *White,* 174 N.E. at 189.

19 *Id.* at 187-89. Although the court does not give the master's name, a newspaper story identifies him as Henry P. Fielding. *See Portia Law School Upheld by Master,* BOSTON GLOBE, Mar. 13, 1930, at 25.

20 *White,* 174 N.E. at 189. *See also Portia Law School Upheld in Dismissal of Student,* BOSTON GLOBE, Jan. 8, 1931, at 13.

After losing her lawsuit, White became a records clerk for the federal government. *See James [sic] A White in the 1940 United States Federal Census, available at* https://www.ancestry.com/discoveryui-content/view/91625699:2442 (listing White's employer as the Works Progress Administration). Curiously, this census identifies White as Native American. In all other available records, she is identified as Black. *See, e.g., 1920 United States Federal Census for Annie J White, available at* https://www.ancestry.com/discoveryui-content/

view/90489443:6061 (Annie was White's middle name). For a further discussion, see SMITH, *supra* note 1 of Chapter 1, at 69 n.74 (Smith summarizes White's case in his chapter "Black Students in White Law Schools").

21 *See* Gulbranson v. Commissioner, T.C. Memo. 1964-313; Kim v. Commissioner, T.C. Memo. 1969-126.

Chapter 3

POST-1970 EXPULSION CASES—
LYING TO GAIN ADMISSION

Every law school's application form now asks whether the applicant has an arrest record, has ever been suspended or expelled by another school, or has committed any act that casts doubt on their fitness to practice law.[1] Applicants who lie face a variety of penalties if caught, including expulsion.[2]

In *Gagne v. Trustees of Indiana University*,[3] for example, Jay C. Gagne lied twice while applying to the defendant's law school at Indianapolis ("IU-I").[4] He also misrepresented his academic career on his resume.[5] When the school discovered his lies, it expelled him.[6] Gagne then sued but lost following a bench trial.[7] In affirming the trial judge's decision, the Indiana Court of Appeals wrote:

> Gagne appeals a negative judgment. Therefore, to prevail on his appeal he must establish that the evidence is without conflict and all reasonable inferences to be drawn from the evidence lead to but one conclusion, yet the trial court reached a different conclusion. . . . The trial court's findings are supported by the evidence, and the findings support the trial court's conclusion. . . .[8]

In *Morris v. Florida Agricultural and Mechanical University*,[9] Brian Morris was expelled after it was discovered that the law school's assistant director of admissions, who was a family friend, along with another employee, had fabricated various documents to help Morris gain admission.[10] When questioned, Morris insisted he knew nothing about the plot.[11]

Following his expulsion, Morris sued and claimed the school had violated Florida law by not giving him a chance to defend himself.[12] Agreeing with this contention, the Florida District Court of Appeal wrote:

> We conclude that Morris was entitled to proper notice and a hearing before he was expelled for alleged fraudulent misconduct regarding his admission to FAMU. Upon remand, Morris must be afforded that to which he is entitled. We express no opinion regarding what the outcome of that hearing should be.[13]

In *Raiser v. Ventura College of Law*,[14] Aaron Raiser was expelled for lying on his application about his dismissal from his prior law school and because he had become a danger to others.[15] When he sued, the district court dismissed his complaint.[16] On appeal, the Ninth Circuit reversed: "That Raiser may have lied on his application for admission does not negate his right to a hearing because the policy manual, which Raiser alleges was part of the contract between himself and Ventura College of Law, provides for a hearing."[17] On remand, the district court found that because of its prior rulings, the only defendant still in the case was Doug Large, the law school's attorney, against whom Raiser had no claim.[18]

In *Brown v. University of Kansas*,[19] Robert M. Brown was expelled after his law school learned about his criminal record.[20] Brown had omitted this information from his application but had updated his form after classes started.[21]

Finding his dismissal proper, the district court rejected Brown's arguments that the procedures used had failed to afford him due process.[22] On appeal, the Tenth Circuit agreed:

For our purposes, the issue is whether greater protections would have proved beneficial. Any benefits would have been minimal in light of the undisputed facts.

These facts include Mr. Brown's acknowledgement that he could be expelled for falsifying his application and his notification to the school that he had given false information. The dean relied on this fact, but gave Mr. Brown an opportunity to respond.

Mr. Brown did so, raising procedural objections and requesting a hearing, but failed to address the fact that he had knowingly provided false information. Accordingly, Dean [Gail B.] Agrawal ordered expulsion.

In light of these undisputed facts, further procedural safeguards would have added little.[23]

In *Bradford v. Regents of the University of North Dakota*,[24] Garet Bradford was expelled after the law school discovered various problems with his application.[25] In response, Bradford sued numerous parties in their official and individual capacities, claiming they had violated his rights under both federal and state law.[26] Although the district court dismissed most of Bradford's complaint, it ruled that some of his constitutional claims could proceed:

Liberally construing Bradford's pro se complaint, the court finds he has stated facially plausible . . . claims against [Dean Kathryn R.L.] Rand, [Assistant Dean Bradley W.] Parrish, [Professor Steven R.] Morrison, and [Professor James M.] Grijalva in their personal capacities. The facts alleged, accepted as true, allow the court to reasonably infer that those individuals' own actions deprived Bradford of his constitutional rights.[27]

In *Cannon v. Southern University Board of Supervisors*,[28] Shaboyd P. Cannon, a third-year law student, was expelled for failing to report two arrests on his application.[29] When Cannon sued, the district court, after various interim rulings,[30] granted the school's motion for summary judgment.[31] On appeal, the Fifth Circuit affirmed:

> Cannon does not challenge the district court's ruling on his equal protection claim. On the due process claim, he argues only that [former law school dean] Freddie Pitcher's deposition testimony raises a material dispute as to whether [Pitcher] was a biased decisionmaker. But Cannon never presented Pitcher's deposition to the district court. In response to Defendants' motion for summary judgment, Cannon submitted just three exhibits—two emails and his own affidavit—all of which the district court found to be inadmissible (a ruling unchallenged by Cannon). . . . Because Pitcher's deposition was not part of the summary judgment record before the district court, we cannot consider it on appeal. And because Cannon offers no other reason to reverse the summary judgment ruling, we affirm.[32]

Lastly, in *Gorbaty v. Mitchell Hamline School of Law,*[33] Howard M. Gorbaty was expelled after the school discovered he had omitted his lengthy criminal record from his application.[34] When confronted, Gorbaty prepared a written account of his crimes.[35] Upon receiving this information, the school revoked its admission offer.[36]

Gorbaty responded by suing the school for breach of contract.[37] In dismissing his complaint for failure to state a claim, the district court wrote:

> Gorbaty asserts that the school did not follow the disciplinary-hearing policy outlined in its handbook and that he was targeted and discriminated against by the school, yet provides no legal authority to support this argument. . . . Even if any authority supported his contention, the application itself plainly stated "an inaccurate or incomplete application may be the basis for denial of admission, or, if I am admitted, for suspension or dismissal from Mitchell Hamline School of Law or revocation of a degree." (Fall 2018 Application at 5.) Thus, Gorbaty fails

to demonstrate the existence of a contract and makes no mention of any condition precedent. The claim thus fails to plausibly allege any elements required for a breach-of-contract claim, and thus Defendant's Motion [to Dismiss] is granted.[38]

1   As has been pointed out elsewhere, such questions are of relatively recent origin. *See* John S. Dzienkowski, *Character and Fitness Inquiries in Law School Admissions,* 45 S. TEX L. REV. 921, 923 (2004) (explaining that as late as the 1980s, few law schools asked such questions). *See also* Law School Admission Council, *Misconduct & Irregularities: Ethical Conduct in Applying to Law School,* at https://www.lsac.org/applying-law-school/misconduct-irregularities (last visited Apr. 1, 2022) (describing the current efforts used by law schools to discover such incidents).

2   Some lies are not discovered until after an applicant has graduated from law school and either has sought to become, or has become, a lawyer. In such cases, courts have not hesitated to impose serious punishment. *See, e.g.,* Attorney Grievance Comm'n of Md. v. Kepple, 68 A.3d 797 (Md.), *later proceedings at In re* Reinstatement of Kepple, 75 A.3d 322 (Md. 2013) (attorney, while a law student at the University of West Virginia, lied repeatedly about where she lived to claim in-state residency and avoid paying an extra $11,050 in tuition—*indefinite suspension of law license); In re* Application of Wilson, 980 N.E.2d 1018 (Ohio 2012) (bar applicant failed to report that he had been academically dismissed from Golden Gate University's law school before earning his law degree at the Detroit College of Law—*permission to take bar exam delayed until July 2014); In re* Rodriguez, 753 N.E.2d 1289 (Ind. 2001) (lawyer failed to report that he had been academically dismissed from both the University of Miami's law school and Nova University's law school before earning his law degree at Ohio Northern University—*90 day suspension of law license*); Florida Bd. of B. Exam'rs *ex rel.* John Doe, 770 So. 2d 670 (Fla. 2000) (bar applicant lied on both his law school application

and bar application regarding numerous incidents, including twice being expelled from an unidentified law school—*bar admission indefinitely denied*).

3   692 N.E.2d 489 (Ind. Ct. App.), *transfer denied*, 706 N.E.2d 167 (Ind. 1998).

4   *Id.* at 491. Gagne applied to IU-I as a freshman, was accepted, but opted to go to John Marshall Law School in Chicago. *Id.* After his first year, he decided to transfer to IU-I. *Id.* IU has two law schools— one in Bloomington (founded 1842) and the other in Indianapolis (founded 1894). *See* Elizabeth R. Osborn, *Indiana Courts and Lawyers, 1816-2004, in* THE HISTORY OF INDIANA LAW 257, 270 (David J. Bodenhamer & Randall T. Shepard eds., 2006).

5   *Gagne,* 692 N.E.2d at 491.

6   *Id.* at 492-93.

7   *Id.* at 491.

8   *Id.* at 493, 496. Following his expulsion, Gagne became a financial advisor. *See Jay Gagne's Education,* CORPBIO, June 15, 2016, *at* http:// jaygagne.corpbio.com/. In 2010, Gagne represented himself after he received a traffic ticket for making an illegal U-turn on an interstate highway. Once again, he lost. *See* Gagne v. State, 952 N.E.2d 289 (Ind. Ct. App. 2011).

9   23 So. 3d 167 (Fla. Dist. Ct. App. 2009).

10 *Id.* at 168. Although the court does not identify them, the two employees were Derrien Bonney and Carol Rojas. *See* Angeline J. Taylor, *FAMU Fires Three After Probe into Law School,* TALLAHASSEE DEMOCRAT, June 13, 2008, at 3A.

11 *Morris,* 23 So. 3d at 169.

12 *Id.*

13 *Id.* at 170. It appears that Morris did not further contest his expulsion and no additional information about him, or his lawsuit, has been located. No information can be obtained from Morris's law-

yer (an Orlando sole practitioner named Joseph Morrell) because he died in 2020. *See Obituaries—Attorney Joseph Morrell, Sr.,* ORLANDO SENTINEL, Nov. 12, 2020, at B5.

14 488 F. App'x 219 (9th Cir. 2012).

The Ventura College of Law, a non-ABA-approved law school, is an accredited California law school (meaning that its graduates can sit for the California bar exam). *See* The Santa Barbara & Ventura Colleges of Law, *About the Santa Barbara & Ventura Colleges of Law, at* https://www.collegesoflaw.edu/about-the-santa-barbara-ventura-colleges-of-law-2/ (last visited Apr. 1, 2022) (under "Accreditation").

15 This information comes from the first of the district court's *thirteen* reported opinions:

> The letter [informing Plaintiff that he had been expelled] stated two reasons for Plaintiff's expulsion: (1) Plaintiff falsified his VCL application by indicating that he had not been terminated from his previous law school and that he was eligible to return to that school; and (2) VCL believed that Plaintiff posed an 'unreasonable risk of harm to [VCL] employees and other [VCL] students.' (FAC Ex. D.) Plaintiff alleges that his application to VCL was not fraudulent because he was eligible to return to his previous school upon meeting with a psychologist. Plaintiff alleges that he simply chose not to meet with the psychologist.

Raiser v. Ventura Coll. of L., Case No. CV 09-00254 RGK (AGRx), 2009 WL 10692054, at *2 (C.D. Cal. July 9, 2009).

16 *See Raiser,* 488 F. App'x at 221.

17 *Id.* at 222. The Ninth Circuit did not address the alternative reason for Raiser's expulsion (*viz.,* posing a danger to others).

18 *See* Raiser v. Ventura Coll. of L., Case No. CV 09-00254-RGK (AGRx), 2014 WL 12774767, at *1 (C.D. Cal. Apr. 18, 2014).

By the time he entered law school, Raiser, who currently is homeless and lives in his car, see Raiser v. San Diego Cnty., Case No.: 19-CV-751-GPC, 2021 WL 5234410, at *1 (S.D. Cal. Nov. 10, 2021), already had become a professional litigant. To date, he has sued the Mormon Church; Brigham Young University; the University of La Verne; Utah and San Diego counties; the municipalities of Fresno, Los Angeles, Murrieta, Provo City, Temecula, and Upland; and numerous judges and other public officials. As a result, Raiser has been declared a "vexatious litigant" by the Ninth Circuit, the District of Utah, the Central District of California, and the California state courts. *See* Raiser v. Casserly, Case No.: 18-CV-1836 JLS (AHG), 2020 WL 8970541, at *3 (S.D. Cal. Feb. 10, 2020).

19 16 F. Supp. 3d 1275 (D. Kan. 2014), *aff'd,* 599 F. App'x 833 (10th Cir. 2015).

20 *Id.* at 836.

21 *Id.* at 835.

22 *Id.* at 836.

23 *Id.* at 837. Since losing his lawsuit, Brown has been working as a real estate consultant. *See Business Entity Search,* STATE OF KANSAS—OFFICE OF THE SECRETARY OF STATE (listing Brown as the owner or president of three Overland Park companies: Realest Solutions Inc., Rents Done Right LLC, and RMB Consulting Group, Inc.).

24 Case No. 2:15-cv-39, 2015 WL 13648357 (D.N.D. Aug. 12, 2015).

25 *Id.* at *2. The court does not indicate the nature of the problems, saying only that the school "listed 'five situations' and asked Bradford to completely describe those situations[.]" *Id.*

26 *Id.* at *1.

27 *Id.* at *4. Following the court's decision, Bradford announced he was going to hire a lawyer and file an amended complaint. By 2018, however, he had not done so, leading the law school to deem the matter closed. *See* North Dakota State Board of Higher Education—

Budget and Finance Committee, *October 16, 2018, Meeting Minutes,* at 11, *available at* 10-16-18-BFC-Meeting-Minutes-Combined.pdf ("Per now aged media reports, Plaintiff intended to dismiss [his] remaining claims without prejudice, retain legal counsel, and re-file. Plaintiff's complaint with the Department of Education, Office of Civil Rights, filed in April 2016, to date remains pending. Plaintiff has not refiled. UND is considering this resolved.").

28 Civil Action 17-527-SDD-RLB, 2018 WL 1881250 (M.D. La. Apr. 19, 2018), *later proceedings at* Civil Action 17-527-SDD-RLB, 2019 WL 1590585 (M.D. La. Apr. 12, 2019), *and later proceedings at* Civil Action 17-527-SDD-RLB, 2019 WL 2656209 (M.D. La. June 27, 2019), *aff'd,* 827 F. App'x 454 (5th Cir. 2020).

29 *Cannon,* 2019 WL 2656209, at *1. The court does not explain the nature of Cannon's arrests. However, a later media report indicates that they were for sexual assault. *See* Janelle McPherson, *Texas Southern's Pay-for-Play Admission Scandal,* NAT'L JURIST, 2020 Back to School Issue, at 10, 11.

30 *See Cannon,* 2018 WL 1881250, at *4 (dismissing Cannon's state law breach of contract claim); *Cannon,* 2019 WL 1590585, at *7 (ordering Cannon to pay deposition-related sanctions).

31 *Cannon,* 2019 WL 2656209, at *7.

32 *Cannon,* 827 F. App'x at 455. Following his expulsion, Cannon was one of seventeen students who bribed their way into Texas Southern University's ("TSU") law school. *See* McPherson, *supra* note 29 of this chapter, at 10, 11. When confronted, Cannon confessed to giving cash ($16,200) and free airline and concert tickets to Edward W. Rene, TSU's assistant dean of admissions and financial aid. *Id.* at 11. After TSU expelled him, Cannon recanted his confession. *Id.*

33 Civ. No. 20-745 (PAM/KMM), 2020 WL 2769148 (D. Minn. May 28, 2020).

34 *Id.* at *1.

35 *Id.* According to the court, Gorbaty provided information about five incidents:

- In 2015, a jury found Gorbaty guilty of harassing communications for sending unwanted Facebook and text messages to a woman. He was sentenced to a fine and 45 days in jail. (Docket No. 7, Ex. B at 13-23.)
- In 2016, he fired two shots from a .38 caliber revolver at his neighbor's residence, and was found guilty of second-degree wanton endangerment. He was sentenced to 12 months' probation. (<u>Id.</u> at 25-29.)
- In 2017, he was sentenced to three days in jail for violating a protective order against the woman to whom he sent harassing communications. (<u>Id.</u> at 31-32.)
- In 2018, Gorbaty was charged with assault for striking his girlfriend's minor daughter and beating her head into the floor. This charge was later dropped. (<u>Id.</u> at 34-40.)
- In 2018, he was charged with again violating the protective order. This charge was also subsequently dropped. (<u>Id.</u> at 42-43.)

Id. (underlining in original). For a further look at Gorbaty's brushes with the law prior to entering law school, see Gorbaty v. Rodriguez, No. 2016-CA-000295-ME, 2017 WL 3669486 (Ky. Ct. App. Aug. 25, 2017).

36 *Gorbaty*, 2020 WL 2769148, at *2.

37 *Id.* at *3. By now, Gorbaty was living in New Jersey. As a result, he sued Mitchell Hamline in a New Jersey state court and claimed "that his omission of the criminal cases were 'minor discrepancies' and concerned 'past youthful indiscretions.'" *See* Charles Toutant, *Aspiring Lawyer Sues Law School After Admission Revoked*, N.J. L.J., Jan. 28, 2019, at 1. After the school removed the case to federal court, the complaint was dismissed for lack of personal jurisdiction. *See* Gorbaty v. Mitchell Hamline Sch. of L., Civil Action No. 18-16691

(ES) (CLW), 2019 WL 3297211, at *4 (D.N.J. July 23, 2019) ("[T]he evidence in this record overwhelmingly shows that none of the relevant activity giving rise to Plaintiff's claims have any connection to New Jersey.").

38 *Gorbaty*, 2020 WL 2769148, at *3.

Chapter 4

POST-1970 EXPULSION CASES—
FINANCIAL ISSUES

Although rare, law students sometimes get expelled for financial issues.[1]

In *DeAngelis v. Widener University School of Law*,[2] for example, Mary Jane DeAngelis was expelled "due to late payment of her tuition and housing bills."[3] In response, she sued the school for disability discrimination under various federal and state laws.[4] The district court found the bulk of her complaint time-barred but ruled she could pursue her housing claim.[5]

After some foot-dragging by DeAngelis,[6] the trial commenced on August 6, 1988.[7] During a break on the first day, DeAngelis and the law school reached a settlement—in exchange for $35,000, DeAngelis agreed to give the school a general release.[8] As soon as the settlement was placed on the record, however, DeAngelis "attempted to renege on her agreement because she wanted to add an additional term compelling defendants to erase her dismissal from her law school records."[9] Finding that DeAngelis could not change the terms of the deal after agreeing to them, the district court refused her request for a modification.[10] On appeal, the Third Circuit summarily affirmed[11] and the U.S. Supreme Court denied her petition for *certiorari*.[12]

In contrast, in *Mason v. Board of Regents of the University of Oklahoma*,[13] law student Perry P. Mason[14] was expelled after it was discovered he had "fail[ed] to report income on his student financial aid application."[15] When Mason's efforts to be reinstated came up short,[16] he sued the school for breach of contract as well as a variety of torts:

employment discrimination (even though he never worked for either the university or the law school); false light; and intentional infliction of emotional distress.[17]

The trial court dismissed Mason's lawsuit for failure to state a claim.[18] In affirming this decision the Oklahoma Court of Civil Appeals wrote:

> After *de novo* review of the record on appeal, we have concluded that Mason can prove no set of facts which would entitle him to relief on any of the causes of action asserted in his amended petition. For this reason, we affirm the trial court's grant of dismissal with prejudice to refiling.[19]

1   For a case in which a student was expelled for poor grades, did not judicially challenge his expulsion, but then tried to use it as a defense when the law school sued him for his final semester's tuition, see Case W. Res. Univ. v. Brandt, No. 39903, 1979 WL 210631 (Ohio Ct. App. Dec. 13, 1979) (affirming order that student pay school $1,400 in outstanding charges).

2   No. Civ. A. 97-6254, 1998 WL 54333 (E.D. Pa. Jan. 13, 1998), *later proceedings at* No. Civ. A. 97-6254, 1998 WL 372420 (E.D. Pa. June 2, 1998), *and later proceedings at* No. Civ. A. 97-6254, 1998 WL 474169 (E.D. Pa. Aug. 4, 1998), *and later proceedings at* 1998 WL 964207 (E.D. Pa. Nov. 3, 1998), *aff'd,* 187 F.3d 625 (3d Cir.), *cert. denied,* 528 U.S. 1053 (1999), *reh'g denied,* 529 U.S. 1034 (2000).

3   *DeAngelis,* 1998 WL 54333, at *1.

4   *Id.* As the court explains, DeAngelis had "a neuromuscular disorder called spinal muscular atrophy [that caused her] weakness, fatigue and other consequences. . . ." *Id.*

5   *Id.* at *3.

6   *See DeAngelis,* 1998 WL 372420, at *2 (rejecting DeAngelis's request to extend discovery); *DeAngelis,* 1998 WL 474169, at *2 (denying DeAngelis's request to postpone the trial).

7   *DeAngelis,* 1998 WL 964207, at *1.

8   *Id.*

9   *Id.*

10 *Id.* at *2.

11 *See DeAngelis,* 187 F.3d at 625.

12 *See DeAngelis*, 528 U.S. at 1053. Since losing her case, DeAngelis has worked as a freelance technical writer in Rhode Island. *See Mary Jane DeAngelis*, LINKEDIN, *at* https://www.linkedin.com/in/mary-jane-deangelis-49963545/ (last visited Apr. 1, 2022).

13 No. CJ 99-2416 L, 2000 WL 35441258 (Okla. Dist. Ct. Feb. 7, 2000), *later proceedings at* No. CJ 99-2416 L, 2000 WL 35441257 (Okla. Dist. Ct. Apr. 3, 2000), *aff'd*, 23 P.3d 964 (Okla. Ct. Civ. App. 2000), *cert. denied*, 534 U.S. 853 (2001).

14 Prior to entering law school, Mason legally changed his name from "Perry Harold Parsin" to "Perry Popeye Mason." *See* "Boots Callahan," *Today I Learned*, REDDIT, *at* https://www.reddit.com/r/today-ilearned/comments/3t3d48/til_a_man_changed_his_name_to_perry_popeye_mason/ (last visited Apr. 1, 2022).

In choosing his new name, Parsin probably did not know that in 1909 Erle Stanley Gardner, the writer who invented the character of attorney Perry Mason, was expelled from Valparaiso University's law school for hitting a faculty member. *See* Albin Krebs, 'The Fiction Factory,' N.Y. TIMES, Mar. 12, 1970, at 1 (quoting Gardner, *id.* at 82, as saying, "I was kicked out for slugging a professor.")

15 *Mason*, 23 P.3d at 966.

16 Following his expulsion, and before taking legal action, Mason made numerous angry appeals to David L. Boren, the university's president. Alarmed by Mason's behavior, Betty L. Baker, Boren's secretary and the target of many of Mason's outbursts, eventually took out a restraining order against him. *See* Baker v. Mason, 958 P.2d 808 (Okla. Ct. Civ. App. 1998).

17 *Mason*, 23 P.3d at 967.

18 *Id.*

19 *Id.* at 971. For an amusing poem about the case, see Robert E. Rains, *The Case of the Vanishing Law Student*, 5 GREEN BAG 2D 463 (2002).

Chapter 5

POST-1970 EXPULSION CASES—POOR GRADES

By far, the largest number of modern reported expulsion cases involves students with grade point averages ("GPA") below the law school's cut-off point, which at most schools is a "2.0" out of a "4.0" (the equivalent of a "C").[1]

In *Grafton v. Brooklyn Law School*,[2] for example, Samuel Grafton and Lyle Silversmith were expelled for poor grades.[3] In response, they filed a reinstatement lawsuit in which they claimed the school had targeted them because they had been staffers on *The Justinian*, the school's student newspaper.[4] Finding that federal jurisdiction did not exist, the district court summarily dismissed the pair's complaint.[5] On appeal, the Second Circuit affirmed:

> Plaintiffs assert that the Law School's conduct violated their constitutional rights to free speech and representation by counsel, guaranteed by the First and Sixth Amendments as made applicable to the states by the Fourteenth, and deprived them of liberty and property without due process of law in violation of the Fourteenth Amendment. There is no need for us to consider the merits of these claims since we hold, as did the district judge, that the actions of the Law School in dismissing and refusing to reinstate the plaintiffs were not "under color of any State Law, statute, ordinance, regulation, custom or usage," 42 U.S.C. § 1983.[6]

In *Abbariao v. Hamline University School of Law*,[7] Abraham C. Abbariao entered the Midwestern School of Law ("MSL") in 1973.[8] It required students to maintain a "70" (on a scale of "0-100"), and after two years Abbariao had a 69.91.[9] At that time, MSL became part of Hamline University and changed its grading scale to "0-4.0."[10] Under this new system, Abbario's 69.91 became a 1.99.[11] Although Hamline required students to maintain a 2.0, it allowed Abbariao to stay in school.[12] When his GPA fell to 1.79 after the first semester of his third year, however, it expelled him.[13]

Abbariao sued for reinstatement, alleging that he had been treated unfairly, but the trial court dismissed his complaint for failure to state a claim.[14] On appeal, the Minnesota Supreme Court decided that Abbariao should have been permitted to pursue his argument that the school had acted in an arbitrary and capricious manner:

> In the instant case, plaintiff was expelled because his cumulative grade point average was below 2.0. But he alleged that his examinations for the fall 1975 semester were singularly graded:
>
> > "That plaintiff has received information believed by him to be true that his examinations in courses taken by him during the Fall, 1975, semester were singled out for special consideration and grading by his professors as the examinations of a 'probationary student' at the direction of defendants and that defendants have otherwise discriminated against him and applied unequal standards without justification in determining his grades."
>
> The import of these allegations is arbitrary and capricious conduct by Hamline officials. As such, they state a claim for relief and the district court erred in holding to the contrary. Plaintiff is entitled to substantiate these and other allegations of arbitrary conduct.[15]

In *Johnson v. Sullivan*,[16] Sandra S. Johnson was expelled after her fourth semester at the University of Montana law school because she was eight points below the school's required minimum GPA.[17] Following a bench trial, a state judge dismissed Johnson's reinstatement lawsuit.[18] On appeal, the Montana Supreme Court affirmed:

> Plaintiff argues that since other students with an academic deficiency have been readmitted, her exclusion [was] unfair. Certainly, not all petitions for readmission are granted. Plaintiff does not argue that the law school faculty should be required to either grant or deny all such petitions. She neither presented nor offered any proof that would tend to show her petition was not given the same consideration that is given to the petitions of other students similarly excluded. Absent any showing of discriminatory or arbitrary treatment by the faculty in their review of her petition for readmission, we must conclude that her contention is groundless and her petition was properly denied.[19]

In *Paulsen v. Golden Gate University*,[20] Richard B. Paulsen, Jr., was expelled after his third year of law school for poor grades.[21] Although the school was willing to let him return as a "non-degree" student and give him a "certificate of attendance," which would have allowed him to take the California bar exam, it was not willing to take him back as a degree student.[22] Paulsen therefore sued to be readmitted as a degree student and won in both the trial court and the appeals court.[23] The California Supreme Court, however, unanimously reversed:

> Paulsen's program was much less rigorous than that required of degree students. The no-degree condition was an explicit recognition that he had not satisfactorily managed the academic rigors of the course load in the degree program, and in the trained judgment of the university would not be able to do so. The fourth year students who continued in the degree program were required to take a minimum of 24 academic units per year; Paulsen, in contrast, struggled with a maximum of 16.

The justification for these limits was fully confirmed by Paulsen's inability to complete more than four units in the second term of his fourth year. To direct that Paulsen receive a degree after he had demonstrated his inability to survive academically under the basic conditions required for other degree students would lead to a judicially mandated erosion of the university's academic standards. . . . The facts thus established that Paulsen's program was an explicit recognition of his demonstrated limitations, and was neither arbitrary nor discriminatory.[24]

In *Shields v. School of Law, Hofstra University,*[25] Candia A. Shields was expelled for poor grades.[26] When she sued, the school moved to have the case dismissed but was rebuffed by the trial court.[27] On appeal, the New York Appellate Division reversed:

[T]here is no basis to conclude that the law school's decision . . . involved anything other than the exercise of sound academic discretion, unfettered by contract and unreviewable by courts. . . .

Since we conclude that plaintiff has not stated a cause of action in contract, we need not address defendants' contention that, on the facts of this case, such a cause of action may be asserted only in a proceeding pursuant to CPLR article 78 and would be governed by the four-month Statute of Limitations generally applicable to such proceedings. . . .

[If, however, Article 78 was available,] we agree with defendants that . . . the proceeding would be time-barred since it was commenced more than four months after plaintiff received final notice of the law school determinations that she was academically ineligible to continue her studies and that her application for a second extension of her conditional advancement had been denied. Plaintiff's request for a reconsideration of these determinations, which was denied on or about July 23, 1979, did not operate to extend the limitations period.[28]

In *Maas v. Corporation of Gonzaga University*,[29] Jan B. Maas, a third-year law student, was expelled after failing to meet the school's 2.2 GPA requirement.[30] Following this dismissal (her third in three years), Maas enrolled in summer school classes at the University of Washington's law school and, when she had accumulated enough credits to graduate from Gonzaga, asked Gonzaga for her degree, which Gonzaga refused to give her.[31]

Maas responded by suing the school for negligence and sought specific performance, but the trial court dismissed her complaint.[32] The Washington Court of Appeals affirmed and explained:

> The decision to award or not award a degree, and based upon what criteria, is one uniquely within the academic sphere. The courts should abstain from interference in this process unless arbitrary and capricious decision making or bad faith is present. . . . We find no evidence of bad faith or an arbitrary and capricious action by the defendant.[33]

In *Marquez v. University of Washington*,[34] Alonzo S. Marquez was expelled after his second year of law school because his GPA was 67.725, just slightly below the school's required 68.[35] In response, Marquez, who was Mexican-American and had been "admitted . . . as a special admittee under [the law school's] affirmative action program,"[36] filed a state lawsuit alleging breach of contract, denial of equal protection, and unspecified acts of discrimination.[37]

The trial court granted the school's motion for summary judgment, the appeals court reversed, and on remand the trial court again granted the school's motion for summary judgment.[38] This time, the Washington Court of Appeals affirmed:

> As the experienced Superior Court judge who ruled on the motions terminating this case in the trial court for the final time summarized it in his oral decision:

Based on the foregoing resume of special academic consider-
ations granted plaintiff and others similarly situated, one must
reach the inescapable conclusion the plaintiff was extended every
reasonable consideration, every reasonable assistance, and every
reasonable opportunity to succeed in law school.

No case has been cited, and the Court is unaware of any rule
of law that would impose a mandate on a public or private educational institution, i.e., University of Washington Law School,
under the circumstances disclosed by this record to assure or
guarantee the "making of a lawyer."

The function of such institutions, and the implementation
of any affirmative action program, is to afford every reasonable
opportunity to such qualified student to succeed. But the major
contribution must, of necessity, be borne by the individual himself
and not by the state.

Motivation; devotion to the law; perseverance; and addiction
to serious studies, are the basic ingredients of anyone seeking
such professional career.[39]

In *Henson v. Honor Committee of U. of Va.*,[40] Josiah D. Henson, a third-
year law student, was expelled because he did not complete multiple
courses.[41] Henson claimed he had been unable to do his schoolwork
because he had been busy defending himself in front of the university's
honor committee in an unrelated proceeding arising from his participa-
tion in a national student organization.[42] When this explanation fell on
deaf ears, he sued the school for violating his due process rights.[43]

The district court granted the school's motion for summary judgment.[44] On appeal, the Fourth Circuit affirmed:

We may easily sympathize with the plight of a student caught up
in extracurricular activities which proved detrimental to his academic
well-being. We may even sense that the misfortunes which ultimately
befell Henson could be disproportionate to whatever his omissions

or transgressions might have been. At the same time, the Law School administration cannot be faulted. It had nothing to do with either the creation of the Honor System at the University or Henson's involvement with it. . . .

The [Law School's] Academic Review Committee exercised its responsibilities in a sympathetic fashion. . . . We cannot judge the reasons [Henson] offers on appeal for [his] failures—that task belongs properly to the law school administrators. The limit of judicial inquiry into academic administration is early reached, and we need not even approach the limit to realize that, as unfortunate as his ultimate position may be, Henson was fairly treated academically.[45]

In *Chezik v. Delaware Law School, Inc.*,[46] Andrew L. Chezik, Jr., a second year student, sought an emergency injunction prohibiting the school from expelling him before he had a chance to take his summer exams.[47] Although his request was granted, his summer grades (an "A-" in Pennsylvania Practice, a "B-" in Lawyering Process, and a "C+" in Professional Responsibility) only brought his GPA up to a 1.947.[48]

When the school moved to expel him, Chezik claimed he had missed raising his GPA to a 2.0 because his Professional Responsibility exam had been graded incorrectly.[49] In finding this argument meritless, the district court wrote:

Plaintiff . . . contends . . . he "took a different test in the Professional Responsibility course than everyone else." In this other test, 27 questions were automatically graded correct, regardless of the answer. Plaintiff alleges that he did not have the benefit of this unique grading advantage and further believes he can prove that the test given to him was either invalid, compared to the test given to the rest of the class, or was incorrectly graded. On this basis, plaintiff claims he has reason to believe that his true cumulative grade point average is 2.00 or above and that he is, therefore, eligible to continue as a student in good standing. However, plaintiff has submitted no evidence whatsoever to substantiate this claim[,] such as a copy of the actual test plaintiff took and a copy of the test "everyone else" supposedly took. In the absence of such evidence, we cannot grant plaintiff any relief.[50]

In *Anderson v. University of Wisconsin,*[51] Fradus L. Anderson, Jr., a Black alcoholic, was expelled after two semesters (spread over three years) because his GPA was 76.92 and the law school required students to have at least a 77 GPA.[52] To gain readmission, Anderson sued the school, claiming it had discriminated against him because of his race and disability.[53]

The district court granted the school's motion for summary judgment.[54] On appeal, the Seventh Circuit affirmed:

> None of the evidence in this record hints that the University held Anderson's race against him. The Law School admitted Anderson under a program permitting minority students to enroll although they do not meet the ordinary criteria; it then twice readmitted Anderson despite his poor performance and drinking problem. Only after he had failed for a third time did the Law School draw the line; even then the Law School permitted Anderson to take a course in the summer session, and the Business School permitted Anderson to take several courses. . . .
>
> [Likewise, n]othing in the record suggests that the University's decision was based on stereotypes about alcoholism as opposed to honest judgments about how Anderson had performed in fact and could be expected to perform. The Law School allowed Anderson to reenter the program twice, knowing that he is an alcoholic; the Business School also allowed Anderson to take courses. In none of his four stints at the University did Anderson perform up to standard.[55]

In *Susan M. v. New York Law School*,[56] Susan Keane[57] was expelled after her second year of law school because her GPA was 1.89.[58] When her efforts to stay in school proved futile, she sued.[59]

The trial court dismissed Keane's petition,[60] but the appellate division held that she should have been given an opportunity to prove that her Corporations grade (a "D") was not the product of "a rational exercise of discretion by the grader."[61] The New York Court of Appeals disagreed and ordered the case dismissed:

> As a general rule, judicial review of grading disputes would inap-
> propriately involve the courts in the very core of academic and educa-
> tional decision making. Moreover, to so involve the courts in assessing
> the propriety of particular grades would promote litigation by count-
> less unsuccessful students and thus undermine the credibility of the
> academic determinations of educational institutions. We conclude,
> therefore, that, in the absence of demonstrated bad faith, arbitrariness,
> capriciousness, irrationality or a constitutional or statutory violation,
> a student's challenge to a particular grade or other academic deter-
> mination relating to a genuine substantive evaluation of the student's
> academic capabilities, is beyond the scope of judicial review. . . .
>
> Petitioner's allegations do not meet this standard; rather, they
> go to the heart of the professor's substantive evaluation of the
> petitioner's academic performance and as such, are beyond judicial
> review. The claim that this Corporations grade resulted in petitioner's
> arbitrary dismissal from the law school was properly dismissed by
> Supreme Court.[62]

In *Gold v. University of Bridgeport School of Law*,[63] Glenn M. Gold was expelled after his first year for poor grades.[64] When his petition for readmission was denied, he sued the school for breach of contract, fraud, and violation of Connecticut's Home Solicitation Sales Act (a consumer protection statute).[65] A jury found the school liable on the breach of contract and fraud counts and awarded Gold $12,000, but the trial judge set aside the jury's verdict for being against the weight of the evidence.[66] In affirming this decision, the Connecticut Court of Appeals wrote in pertinent part:

> From our review of the plaintiff's evidence, we are satisfied that the trial court correctly ruled that there was no basis upon which the jury could conclude that the plaintiff had sustained his burden of proving that he was misled or deceived by the defendants' misrepresentations concerning the law school or its teaching services.[67]

In *Radcliff v. Landau*,[68] Arthur Radcliff was expelled from the University of West Los Angeles[69] after he failed two courses.[70] Claiming that he had been treated more harshly than other students because he was Black and had been active in the Black Law Student Association,[71] Radcliff challenged his expulsion in federal court.[72]

The district court dismissed Radcliff's complaint for lack of subject matter jurisdiction,[73] but the Ninth Circuit reversed.[74] On remand, the district court granted summary judgment in favor of the school.[75] In agreeing with this outcome, the Ninth Circuit explained:

> The district court found that Radcliff's dismissal was mandatory because he had failed two courses. Radcliff failed to allege that students failing more than one course remained in school and presented no evidence that would support such an allegation. The defendants, on the other hand, have presented evidence demonstrating that the law school has a policy of mandatory dismissal upon a student's failure in any first-year course. This evidence consists of the law school student handbook's statement ("A failure in any course will result in dismissal"), and affidavits from various law school administrators to this effect. Given this evidence and the absence of evidence to the contrary, the district court properly entered summary judgment in the defendants' favor.[76]

In *Nolan v. University of South Carolina*,[77] Wendell L. Nolan was expelled after he twice failed his first year of law school.[78] Contending that he had been discriminated against because he was Black, and further contending that he had been the victim of a faculty conspiracy, Nolan filed a federal lawsuit.[79] In granting the school summary judgment, the district court wrote:

> The Magistrate Judge has reviewed the evidence of record and observes that although the plaintiff has alleged that he was denied due process and equal protection because the defendants treated him differently than other students had been treated, plaintiff has not presented any evidence of that alleged fact. The Magistrate Judge also observes that plaintiff has failed to produce any evidence of a conspiracy among faculty members to improperly grade his examination papers and that the record contains no evidence of discrimination based upon the plaintiff's race. Finally, the Magistrate Judge observes that the only evidence in the record is that the plaintiff was afforded all of the opportunities available to a student who fails to maintain the required grade average; that the plaintiff was terminated as a student because he failed to maintain the required grade average; that plaintiff was afforded the established procedures for readmission and was readmitted even though his first year grades were below the required minimum standard; that after repeating the first year of law school, the plaintiff again failed to meet minimum required academic grades; that plaintiff was then allowed to present his petition to the law school faculty and attempt to obtain a two-thirds vote which would have, if successful, permitted him to continue as a law student but he failed to obtain the necessary two-thirds vote and was therefore not readmitted to the law school.
>
> The Court concludes that upon consideration of the pleadings, the evidence of record, the Magistrate Judge's report and recommendation and the objections, together with the arguments thereon, the recommendation must be and it is hereby approved.[80]

On appeal, the Fourth Circuit made even shorter work of Nolan's lawsuit:

Wendell Nolan appeals from the district court's order denying relief under 42 U.S.C. § 1983 (1988). Our review of the record and the district court's opinion accepting the recommendation of the magistrate judge discloses that this appeal is without merit. Accordingly, we affirm on the reasoning of the district court.[81]

In *McGregor v. Louisiana State University Board of Supervisors*,[82] Robert T. McGregor, a disabled student, was expelled after he "repeatedly failed to achieve a passing cumulative GPA and after the Law Center refused to allow [him] to advance to the junior year."[83] Believing that the school had not worked hard enough to accommodate his disabilities,[84] McGregor sued it under both federal and state law.[85] Finding that the school had done all it reasonably could do to help him, the district court granted its motion for summary judgment.[86] On appeal, the Fifth Circuit affirmed:

Viewing the undisputed facts, we can conclude only that the Law Center reasonably accommodated McGregor's disability and that the additional accommodations, if granted, would constitute preferential treatment and go beyond the elimination of disadvantageous treatment. . . . We agree with Judge Duplantier that despite the reasonable accommodations provided, McGregor did not achieve the minimum cumulative GPA as required under the academic standards set by the Law Center. McGregor, therefore, is not an otherwise qualified individual who has been denied the benefits of the Law Center's program solely because of his handicap.[87]

In *Johnson v. Detroit College of Law*,[88] Robert Johnson was expelled after his first year for poor grades.[89] When he sued for readmission, the district court granted the school's motion for summary judgment.[90] On appeal, the Sixth Circuit affirmed in a brief order:

> Seeking monetary damages, injunctive relief, a declaratory judgment, and other relief, Johnson asserted six theories of relief including allegations of handicap and racial discrimination. His argument was that he was not called on to recite or "brief" cases in class with enough regularity to enhance his understanding of the subject matter. He contends that his lack of participation was the result of race and handicap discrimination. Conversely, when he was called on to participate, Johnson alleges that he was ridiculed as a result of his handicap and race. In other words, Johnson argues that had he not been treated as rudely as he alleges, he would have participated more in class, would have learned more and would have been better able to earn passing grades. . . .
>
> Upon review, we conclude that the district court did not err. Johnson can show no genuine issue of material fact that he was the victim of either racial or handicap discrimination, and his allegation that he would have earned higher grades had he not been discouraged from class participation is too speculative to overcome a properly supported motion for summary judgment. . . . Johnson's remaining allegations of error are meritless.[91]

In *Robinson v. Hamline University,*[92] Albert D. Robinson was expelled at the end of his first year because his GPA (1.571) was below the law school's required minimum GPA (1.75).[93] Believing he had been discriminated against because he was Black and learning disabled, Robinson filed a complaint with the Minnesota Department of Human Rights.[94] Finding that the school had acted properly, an administrative law judge dismissed Robinson's complaint.[95] In affirming this decision, the Minnesota Court of Appeals explained: "Robinson failed to provide evidence demonstrating that he could meet Hamline's academic requirements. The ALJ did not err when it concluded that Hamline's decision not to readmit Robinson was not discriminatory."[96]

In *Megenity v. Stenger*,[97] Mark Megenity was expelled from the University of Louisville's law school during his third year for poor grades.[98] In an effort to be readmitted, Megenity claimed that his "D" in Domestic Relations was the result of a "fatally flawed" examination.[99]

After exhausting his administrative remedies, Megenity filed a civil rights lawsuit against the school.[100] A magistrate judge's recommendation that the school be granted summary judgment was adopted by the district court.[101] On appeal, the Sixth Circuit affirmed: "Even if we were to assume that Megenity had a substantive due process right not to be expelled for an arbitrary or capricious reason, defendants here were entitled to summary judgment."[102] In a brief concurrence, Senior Circuit Judge Brown wrote:

> I have no problem in concurring in the result reached by the majority opinion.
>
> I do, however, disagree with the implication (though not the holding) of the majority opinion that the appellant, Megenity, did not have a substantive due process right not to be dismissed from the law school for arbitrary or capricious reasons.[103]

In *Sage v. CUNY Law School*,[104] Cynthia Sage was expelled after she received a failing grade in one of her law school's clinic programs.[105] The trial judge refused Sage's request for an order directing the school to change her grade and reinstate her.[106] On appeal, the New York Appellate Division affirmed:

> Determinations regarding a student's academic qualifications rest upon the subjective professional judgments of trained educators. . . . On the present record before this court, we find no evidence that the respondent's professional judgment was rendered in an arbitrary and

capricious manner. Thus, the petition fails to state a legally cognizable cause of action and was properly dismissed. . . .[107]

In *Murphy v. Franklin Pierce Law Center,*[108] Nancy D. Murphy, a third-year student, was expelled after receiving a string of poor grades.[109] In her readmission lawsuit, Murphy claimed the school had discriminated against her because she was a woman with a disability (diplopia, better known as double vision).[110] Deciding that the real reason she had been expelled was because she lacked the analytical skills needed to do well,[111] the district court granted the school's motion for summary judgment.[112] On appeal, the First Circuit affirmed:

> We . . . conclude . . . as a matter of law [that] Murphy was not other-wise qualified for retention as a student at the Law Center. That is, even with the accommodations provided by the [school's Academic Standing Committee], she was unable to meet both the Law Center's degree requirements and the terms of her probation.[113]

In *Girsky v. Touro College, Jacob D. Fuchsberg Law Center,*[114] Jeffrey Girsky was expelled after his second year for poor grades.[115] When he sued, the trial court ordered the school to hold further proceedings.[116] In reversing this decision and dismissing the case, the New York Appellate Division wrote:

> It is well established that judicial review of the determinations of educational institutions as to the academic performance of their students is limited to the question whether the challenged determination was arbitrary and capricious, irrational, made in bad faith, unconstitutional, or contrary to statute. . . .
>
> Here, the record reveals that the petitioner failed to demonstrate that the challenged determination was arbitrary or capricious or in disregard of the Law Center's own rules and regulations. The petitioner failed Civil Procedure I in his first semester, causing the

school to inform him of its dissatisfaction with his progress. In the succeeding semesters the petitioner also failed Constitutional Law II, performed lower than average in other courses, and did not complete other courses. . . .[117]

In *Kunkel v. Widener University School of Law*,[118] Kenneth J. Kunkel was expelled after his first year because his GPA was 1.7875, which was below the school's required minimum GPA (1.8).[119] When his request for readmission was denied, Kunkel filed a § 1983 lawsuit against the school claiming that it had "deprived [him] of his right to procedural and substantive due process under the Fourteenth Amendment to the United States Constitution."[120]

Although Kunkel's initial complaint was dismissed for failure to state a claim,[121] a motion to dismiss his amended complaint for the same reason was denied.[122] Nearly a year of discovery then followed, after which the court granted the school's motion for summary judgment:

> There is no evidence proffered of the alleged nexus existing between the state and the Law School. Plaintiff has not pointed to any evidence that would support a finding of coercive power of the state exercised over the Law School. Nor has plaintiff identified any evidence that would support a finding that the Law School's actions were within the exclusive prerogative of the State. Summary judgment must be granted because plaintiff cannot prevail on an equal protection or substantive due process claim against the defendant without evidence to support a finding of state action by the Law School.[123]

In *Gill v. Franklin Pierce Law Center*,[124] Robert D. Gill, a third-year student, was expelled after accumulating twelve credits below "C-" (the school's rules permitted students to have no more than nine such credits).[125] Claiming that the school had failed to accommodate his disability—post-traumatic stress disorder caused by growing up in an alcoholic home—Gill sued for readmission.[126] In granting summary judgment for the school, the district court wrote:

> [T]he evidence submitted by defendant establishes that FPLC did not know, and had no reason to know, that plaintiff had a disability for which he required reasonable accommodations. Further, in response to defendant's properly supported motion, plaintiff has failed to submit any evidence to create a genuine issue as to whether FPLC knew or had reason to know of his disability and of his corresponding need for reasonable accommodations.
>
> Under these circumstances, the court finds that FPLC cannot be held liable. . . .[127]

In *Perez v. Hastings College of the Law*,[128] Jonathan D. Perez was expelled twice for poor grades.[129] When the school refused to let him in a third time, he obtained a preliminary injunction ordering his readmission.[130] In reversing this decision, the California Court of Appeal wrote:

> Respondent is not the first student excluded from readmission to the college for failure to meet its academic standards, and if historical precedent is any indicator he won't be the last. The dispositive issue for us is whether the courts or the college should determine whether he was entitled to be readmitted. . . .
>
> Grades are the yardstick for performance in all academic institutions, and failure to maintain satisfactory grades is cause for expulsion or denial of readmission by any standard. Therefore, the school was justified in dismissing respondent for failing to maintain a passing GPA, and offering no evidence of an extraordinary or compelling circumstance excusing his failure.[131]

In *Scott v. Western State University College of Law,*[132] Darryl Scott filed a disability discrimination lawsuit after he was expelled for poor grades.[133] Finding his complaint baseless, the district court granted the school's motion for summary judgment.[134] On appeal, the Ninth Circuit affirmed:

> WSU dismissed Scott after his first year of law school because he failed to maintain the required grade point average ("GPA"). Scott wrote a series of letters seeking readmission. In his third letter to defendant, nearly five months after his dismissal, Scott first mentioned his alleged disability. . . .
>
> Because Scott did not maintain the GPA required to continue at WSU, it is indisputable that he was not "otherwise qualified for the services sought." . . . . In addition, because Scott was dismissed before WSU knew about his alleged disability, he was clearly not excluded solely by reason of his disability. . . .
>
> Because Scott failed to state a prima facie case of disability discrimination under either the ADA or the Rehabilitation Act, we affirm the district court's summary judgment for defendant. . . .
>
> Defendant has requested attorney fees on appeal pursuant to 42 U.S.C. § 12205, on the basis that Scott's claims are frivolous. Defendant's request is denied.[135]

In *Waller v. Southern Illinois University,*[136] James E. Waller was expelled for poor grades.[137] Thereafter, "[t]he university refused to consider readmitting [Waller] because a rule of [the] law school forbids the readmission of a student who flunked out with a grade point average below a certain level and [Waller's] average was below that level."[138] When Waller sued, claiming that the school was required to consider his application for readmission, the district court dismissed his complaint for failure to state a claim.[139] On appeal, the Seventh Circuit affirmed:

The contractual right claimed here . . . is not a right to admission or readmission; it is merely a right to be considered for readmission; and it may be doubted whether that right has sufficient value or definiteness to come within the concept of constitutional property. But as the issue is not discussed by the parties and there is no case on the question, we shall assume for the sake of argument that even so nebulous and etiolated an "entitlement" can be thought of as property. . . .

Even so, the plaintiff has no case, for he has misunderstood the [ABA's] standards [governing law schools], generating a spurious conflict with the law school's rule on readmission. The purpose of [ABA] Standard 505 is simply to assure the school that it need not, to retain its accreditation, adopt a blanket rule of never readmitting a student that it has flunked out. This is apparent from comparison with the ABA's Standard 501(b), which provides that "a law school shall not admit applicants who do not appear capable of satisfactorily completing its educational program and being admitted to the bar." Standard 505 backstops this basic norm by making clear that the law school is not permitted to readmit a student who by flunking out has proved that his admission was in violation of 501(b). There is no implication that the school may not raise the hurdle to readmission higher. Indeed, there is nothing in the standards to suggest that the law school must consider readmitting a student who has flunked out. And surely at the very least the standard permits the school to particularize the vague limitation that the standard imposes on readmissions, and this is what SIU's law school has done in forbidding the readmission of a student whose academic performance is as abysmal as the plaintiff's was. As it is plain that the law school did not violate its contract with the plaintiff, and as his other claims are frivolous, the suit was properly dismissed.[140]

In *Bittle v. Oklahoma City University*,[141] Paul B. Bittle was expelled for poor grades after his third semester.[142] Blaming the law school generally, and his constitutional law professor Charles L. Cantrell specifically, for his poor performance, Bittle filed a multi-count state lawsuit.[143] Without stating its reasons, the trial court granted the school's motion to dismiss.[144] After reviewing the record, the Oklahoma Court of Civil Appeals affirmed:

> Notwithstanding his protestations to the contrary, all of Bittle's claims for fraud, breach of contract, tortious breach of contract, negligence, and unjust enrichment commonly allege a willful or negligent failure of OCU to provide him an adequate legal education as OCU implicitly agreed by admitting him and accepting his payment of tuition, and Bittle has failed to identify or present evidence of any OCU brochure, policy, advertisement or other matter which might reasonably establish a specific agreement for the provision of particular services—beyond the provision of basic education services—as to render OCU's failure in some enumerated particular actionable as a breach of contract. We therefore hold Bittle, in his alternative tort and contract claims, presented neither any recognized legal theory of recovery, nor sufficient facts under any recognized legal theory, and conclude the trial court properly granted judgment to OCU . . . on Bittle's claims of fraud, breach of contract, tortious breach of contract, negligence, and unjust enrichment.
>
> As to Bittle's due process claim, . . . Bittle does not dispute that his continued enrollment at OCU was conditioned on maintenance of a cumulative grade point average at or above that set by OCU policy. In this respect, neither the allegations of Bittle's petition nor the evidentiary materials offered on summary judgment establish any cognizable "state action" either guaranteeing Bittle an education at OCU, or regulating permissible discipline by OCU, as to invoke constitutional due process protections. Moreover, Bittle admits OCU afforded him post-dismissal administrative review, and during that process, the authorities agree Bittle is not entitled to the full panoply of constitutional due process protections. Bittle therefore forwards no actionable violation of the due process clauses of the Fourteenth Amendment

to the United States Constitution or of Art. II, § 7 of the Oklahoma Constitution in the present case.[145]

In *Allison v. Howard University*,[146] Albert Allison, a third-year law student, was expelled after he received an "F" in his 12-credit clinic course.[147] After unsuccessfully petitioning the school for readmission for two years, Allison filed a multi-count complaint in federal court.[148] In granting the school's motion for summary judgment, the court held that Allison's breach-of-contract claims either were time-barred[149] or non-justiciable.[150] As for his claims alleging negligence, improper state action, and disability discrimination, the court found that Allison had failed to produce even a "scintilla" of evidence to support them.[151]

In *Rosenberg v. Golden Gate University, Inc.*,[152] Jordan Rosenberg was expelled after his second year because his "required courses" GPA had fallen below the law school's 2.05 cut-off.[153] When he failed to convince the school to readmit him,[154] Rosenberg sued the school for breach of contract and unfair business practices.[155] He also moved for a preliminary injunction compelling the school to readmit him during the pendency of his lawsuit.[156] This request was denied by the trial court[157] and subsequently affirmed by the California Court of Appeal.[158] In the meantime, the trial court granted the school's motion for summary judgment:

> Rosenberg dispute[s] [his] disqualification, claiming that his minimum GPA was miscalculated. He assert[s] that certain courses from the elective litigation program should have been defined as "required courses" and included in the calculation of minimum GPA for required courses. Rosenberg's novel calculation of minimum GPA [is] not supported by the Academic Standards guidelines contained in the Student Handbook, and Golden Gate declined to accept Rosenberg's interpretation of what constitutes a "required course" for purposes of the minimum GPA requirement of 2.05. . . .

Rosenberg claims that Golden Gate violated its policies because Dean [Sue] Schechter did not exercise "informed discretion" in reviewing his request for a variance from the grade requirements. The declaration of Dean Schechter establishes otherwise. Dean Schechter spent considerable time considering Rosenberg's request for a variance and did exercise her discretion in denying his request. ... She reviewed the criteria set forth in the Student Handbook and determined that a variance in Rosenberg's case was inappropriate. He did not meet the criteria for a variance, in part because his academic deficiencies were not caused by a situation beyond his control. ...

[In short,] Rosenberg presents no evidence demonstrating that the Dean violated any policies regarding academic review or that Golden Gate acted arbitrarily in applying its review policies to him.[159]

In *Marlon v. Western New England College*,[160] Dianne Marlon, who suffered from carpal tunnel syndrome ("CTS"), was expelled twice for poor grades.[161] When the law school refused to give her a third chance, she sued it for disability discrimination.[162] Finding that Marlon had failed to prove that her CTS made her a disabled person, the district court granted the school's motion for summary judgment.[163] On appeal, the First Circuit, in a brief opinion, affirmed because "Marlon has failed to raise a material issue of fact that she was disabled under the relevant statutes."[164]

In *Goehring v. Chapman University*,[165] Dennis Goehring was expelled with a 1.959 GPA.[166] At the time of his expulsion, Goehring had completed 74 of the 88 credits he needed to graduate.[167]

During Goehring's attendance at Chapman, the law school had tried, without success, to obtain ABA approval.[168] Believing they had been duped, Goehring and two other students sued the school for fraudulently misrepresenting its accreditation status.[169]

Because Goehring had flunked out and the other students had not,[170] the trial court severed Goehring's claims and granted summary judgment to the school.[171] In affirming its decision to do so, the California Court of Appeal wrote:

> Th[e] evidence shows Goehring's damages were not caused by the alleged misrepresentations that induced him to attend Chapman, but by his academic dismissal. Indeed, Goehring concedes that but for his dismissal, he "would have received his degree from an ABA-approved law school."
>
> . . . .
>
> Goehring asserts he raised triable issues of fact regarding whether he actually "flunked out," and the court improperly weighed the evidence on the reasons for his dismissal. However, his complaint was not based on wrongful dismissal, but on false representations that induced him to enroll and reenroll in Chapman. He produced no evidence to support a finding he suffered damages as a result of relying on those misrepresentations, likely an insurmountable task given his academic dismissal. Contrary to Goehring's assertion, the fact that other plaintiffs proceeded to trial does not show he raised an issue of material fact requiring trial.[172]

In *Jackson v. Kim*,[173] Robert Jackson was expelled from Texas Southern University's law school after his first year for poor grades.[174] Jackson attributed his expulsion to the zero Professor J. Faith Jackson had given him on his "closed memo" in her Lawyering Process I course. Professor Jackson had assigned Jackson a zero after discovering he had violated her instructions by sharing his memo with a fellow student named Jong W. Kim.[175]

When Jackson sued the school for breach of contract, defamation, due process violations, and fraud, the trial court granted its motion for summary judgment.[176] Forsaking the rest of his complaint, Jackson appealed only the denial of his due process claims.[177] In affirming the trial court, the Texas Court of Appeals wrote:

> Jackson's entire claim is that his due process rights were violated because TSU did not follow its own rules, and that he had a substantive interest in the process itself. Notably, he does not assert that the process he was given did not meet minimum due process standards.
>
> Following the reasoning of *Olim [v. Wakinekona*, 461 U.S. 238 (1983),] we conclude that Jackson has failed to state a cognizable due process claim because he has no substantive interest in specific rules.
>
> . . .
>
> Reading his brief very generously, Jackson's brief also raises a substantive due process claim. Specifically, he claims he has the right to have his writing assignment fairly graded. He argues that . . . his grade of zero is more likely to be found arbitrary and unreasonable if this court is precluded from considering the fact that the zero was given as punishment for cheating. . . .
>
> Giving a student a zero for cheating on course work is not irrational. It is a logical punishment, often handed down by teachers, for turning in work that is not one's own, or for helping another person turn in work that is not their own. It is rational in that it gives no credit to a student who may not have done any work himself, and it is rational in that it serves as a deterrent to keep students from engaging in or repeating academic dishonesty. Jackson was not denied substantive due process in his receipt of a zero for cheating.[178]

In *Howell v. University of West Los Angeles School of Law,*[179] Joan M. Howell was expelled after her first semester, during which she earned a GPA (1.68) that was below the score needed to stay in school on probation (1.85).[180] When her petition for reinstatement was denied,[181] Howell sued the school for breach of contract, intentional and negligent infliction of emotional distress, and negligent misrepresentation.[182]

The trial court granted summary judgment in favor of the school.[183] In affirming this decision, the California Court of Appeal explained: "With respect to each cause of action, UWLA met its burden of showing Howell cannot establish at least one element. Howell did not show a triable issue of fact with respect to any cause of action. Accordingly, summary judgment was proper."[184]

In *Peebles v. University of Dayton*,[185] Eric M. Peebles was expelled after his first semester of law school because his GPA (1.00) was below the cut-off point (1.60) for staying enrolled on probation.[186] When his petition for readmission was denied, Peebles, who suffered from spastic cerebral palsy, filed an administrative complaint with the Ohio Civil Rights Commission ("OCRC").[187] Although a deal permitting Peebles to take classes as an auditor was worked out, it unraveled after the parties failed to reach a settlement agreement.[188] Peebles then sued the school in federal court for disability discrimination.[189]

The school moved to dismiss Peebles's complaint on the basis of *Younger* abstention.[190] In granting the school's motion, the district court wrote:

> Generally, abstention is appropriate under *Younger* if: 1) state judicial proceedings are ongoing; 2) the state proceedings implicate important state interests; and 3) the state proceedings afford an adequate opportunity to raise federal questions. . . . Plaintiffs properly concede that the answer to the first two inquiries is yes; therefore, the controversy only arises with respect to the third element. . . .
>
> [T]he Court has reviewed O.R.C. Chapter 4112 and has not found any clear statutory bar to Plaintiffs' assertion of ADA or Rehabilitation Act charges before the OCRC. . . . Second, the Court is aware of two cases in which a plaintiff filed a charge with the OCRC alleging disability discrimination under the ADA. . . . This establishes that Plaintiff could have filed a charge of discrimination under the ADA with the OCRC. Furthermore, O.R.C. § 4112.06 allows for state court review of the OCRC's actions.

Additionally, the Ohio Supreme Court [has] held that state courts have concurrent jurisdiction with federal courts over Rehabilitation Act claims. . . .

Accordingly, all three prongs for *Younger* abstention are satisfied and the Court GRANTS Defendants' motion to dismiss.[191]

In *Kiani v. Trustees of Boston University*,[192] law student Layla Kiani was suspended six days before she was supposed to graduate on suspicion of plagiarism.[193] When the dust finally settled seven months later, Kiani had been found guilty; three of her grades had been lowered; and she had been expelled because her GPA now was below a 2.0.[194] When her petition for readmission was denied, Kiani filed a 10-count complaint in state court.[195]

The school removed the case to federal court, where seven of Kiani's counts were dismissed.[196] Subsequently, the school moved for summary judgment on the three remaining counts, which alleged, respectively, breach of contract, violation of the ADA, and violation of the Rehabilitation Act.[197] Deeming the motion to be well founded, the magistrate judge recommended that it be granted.[198] In a one-sentence order, the district court adopted the magistrate judge's suggestion.[199]

In *Buck v. Thomas M. Cooley Law School*,[200] Nahzy A. Buck was expelled after her third semester because her GPA was 1.43.[201] When her petition for readmission was denied, Buck filed a four-count complaint in state court.[202]

The trial court granted Buck's request for a temporary restraining order ("TRO"), which allowed her to resume school.[203] Subsequently, Buck stipulated to the dismissal of her fourth count (denial of due process).[204] The school then moved for summary judgment on Buck's remaining claims.[205] Although the court granted the school's motion on two of them (breach of fiduciary duty and violation of the state's consumer protection statute),[206] it held that the school was liable under Michigan's Persons With Disabilities Civil Rights Act ("PWDCRA") because it "had misled plaintiff with regard to the existence of her disability."[207]

Finding that the trial court had misread the statute, the Michigan Court of Appeals reversed:

> [T]he trial court concluded that defendant should have handled plaintiff's complaints of being "slow" and nervous by [either] doing nothing or referring her to a professional, such as a psychologist. It ignored the fact that nothing in the PWDCRA requires this procedure and that plaintiff was in the best position to determine the possible existence or extent of a disability. . . . Before plaintiff provided documentation of a disability and requested an accommodation, defendant had no statutory duty to act on behalf of plaintiff. Because the PWDCRA does not impose a duty on defendant to properly diagnose an alleged learning disability, there is no genuine issue of material fact regarding this issue, and defendant was entitled to judgment as a matter of law.[208]

In *Dulemba v. Thomas M. Cooley Law School*,[209] Jennifer L. Dulemba was expelled for poor grades on September 18, 2002.[210] On September 19, 2005 (the 18th being a Sunday), she sued the school for disability discrimination.[211] The clerk, however, did not file her complaint because it was not signed.[212] After Dulemba fixed her mistake, the clerk filed the complaint on September 27, 2005.[213]

Believing the lawsuit to be time barred due to the state's three-year statute of limitations, the school moved for, and was granted, a dismissal.[214] In affirming this decision, the Michigan Court of Appeals wrote:

> Here, the clerk properly rejected the unsigned complaint. The later signing of the complaint cannot somehow transform this rejection into a "filing" for purposes of the statute of limitations. The trial court properly granted summary disposition to defendant.

Plaintiff additionally argues on appeal that the court erred in concluding that plaintiff failed to exhaust her administrative remedies. In light of our above conclusion, we need not address this argument.[215]

In *Kodatt v. Oklahoma City University*,[216] Shelly L. Kodatt was expelled after two full-time semesters and two-part time semesters because "she was unable to maintain the requisite grade point minimum of 4.50 [on a 12-point scale]."[217] To gain readmission, Kodatt filed a disability discrimination lawsuit.[218] After extensive motion practice,[219] Kodatt's claims were "confined to her complaints about her grade in Professor [Carla] Spivack's Fall 2005 Legal Profession class."[220] According to Kodatt, Spivack had graded Kodatt's exam differently than she had graded the exams of non-disabled students.[221] Insisting that Kodatt simply was unqualified to be a law student, the school moved for summary judgment.[222] In granting its request, the court wrote:

> [T]here is no evidence before the Court that Plaintiff ever disclosed to
> Professor Spivack prior to taking the Legal Profession Exam that she
> was to receive extra or double time to take the exam or that Professor
> Spivack knew until after she had graded Plaintiff's exam and Plaintiff
> had appealed her grade that the examination in question was that of
> a person with a disability who had been accorded extra time to take
> the exam and/or that it was Plaintiff's exam. Accordingly, Plaintiff has
> wholly failed to present evidence that Professor Spivack and/or OCU
> intentionally discriminated against Plaintiff because of her disability or
> that OCU was deliberately indifferent to a strong likelihood that pursuit
> of its policies would likely result in a violation of Plaintiff's rights
> under the ADA and/or Rehabilitation Act.[223]

On appeal, the Tenth Circuit, after granting Kodatt's request to prosecute her appeal under the pseudonym "Jane Doe,"[224] affirmed:

[A]ll of the evidence of record, viewed in the light most favorable to Ms. Doe, supports OCU Law School's position that it dismissed Ms. Doe solely because of her poor academic performance. We therefore agree with the district court that Ms. Doe's evidence does not create a fact issue as to whether she was discriminated against because of her disability.[225]

In *Brodsky v. New England School of Law*,[226] Seva Brodsky, a second-year student, was expelled after he failed two courses (Constitutional Law and Criminal Law).[227] When the school refused to readmit him, he sued in state court for breach of contract, disability discrimination under both federal and state law, and violation of the Massachusetts Consumer Protection Act.[228] The school removed the case to federal court and then moved for dismissal.[229] Although the court granted the school's motion as to the breach of contract and consumer protection counts,[230] it refused to do so on the disability discrimination counts:

Although Brodsky has at least alleged a disability that substantially limits his ability to learn, the Court notes that he faces a substantial obstacle in proving the same. In particular, it is less than clear how Brodsky's poor "executive functioning" and memory abilities impacted his performance in two law school classes but not others. Nevertheless, Brodsky is not required to make such a showing at the pleading stage. . . .

Consequently, Brodsky's ADA, Rehabilitation Act and MERA [Massachusetts Equal Rights Act] claims will not be dismissed.[231]

In *Oser v. Capital University Law School*,[232] Andrew M. Oser was expelled after his first year with a 1.82 GPA.[233] When his petition for reinstatement was turned down, he sued the school for disability discrimination under federal and state law, claiming that it had failed to accommodate his ADHD.[234]

Oser also moved for a TRO and a preliminary injunction to be able to attend classes while his lawsuit was being heard.[235] In refusing to grant these requests, the court wrote:

> A plaintiff seeking a preliminary injunction must demonstrate that: (1) there is a substantial likelihood that the plaintiff will prevail on the merits; (2) the plaintiff will suffer irreparable injury without the injunction; (3) the balance of hardships tips in the plaintiff's favor; and (4) the injunction serves the public interest. . . .
>
> None of the factors weigh in favor of granting a preliminary injunction in this case. The balance of hardships in this case, as well as the public interest, however, do not point very strongly in Capital's favor. Nevertheless, the Court finds it most problematic that Oser has not established a likelihood of success on the merits and has not shown that he will suffer any irreparable harm in the absence of an injunction. This Court concludes that the extraordinary remedy of a preliminary injunction is not warranted based on the circumstances of this case.[236]

In *Meisenhelder v. Florida Coastal School of Law, Inc.*,[237] Judith K. Meisenhelder was expelled after four years of on-again/off-again attendance because of poor grades.[238] When her petition for readmission was denied, Meisenhelder filed a two-count federal disability discrimination lawsuit.[239] In granting the school's motion for summary judgment, the district court explained:

> It is not disputed that Plaintiff suffers from a number of medical conditions that could be regarded individually as impairments. . . .
>
> Plaintiff was taking a variety of medications to help manage her impairments. As a result, her condition was improving by the fall of 2007, as noted by her doctor. Moreover, during the next two semesters, spring and summer 2008, Plaintiff did not have any issues with class attendance. Plaintiff was only dismissed from the school during

summer 2008, after her G.P.A. again fell below the required 2.0. Until that point, and even during the height of her difficulties, Plaintiff managed to keep her G.P.A. within the required range. As Plaintiff has failed to establish that she suffered from a disability as defined by the ADA or Section 504, her case cannot go forward.[240]

On appeal, the Eleventh Circuit, in a short opinion, affirmed:

> The district court's summary judgment order lays out the salient facts regarding appellant's relationship with appellee's law school over a period that extended from the fall of 2004 to her dismissal from the school in the late summer of 2008. The district court concluded, on the basis of those facts, that appellant failed to establish that she suffered from a disability as defined by the ADA or Section 504. The court went one step further and assuming that appellant had established such disability, she failed to show that appellee failed reasonably to accommodate it.
>
> We discern no error in the district court's disposition of appellant's claims. We therefore affirm its judgment.[241]

In *Shapiro v. Abraham Lincoln University School of Law*,[242] Joshua B. Shapiro was expelled after he failed the state's "Baby Bar Exam" three times.[243] In response, he brought a multi-count complaint against the school alleging, among other things, that it had failed to accommodate his learning disability.[244] Following extensive motion practice,[245] the trial court granted the school's motion for summary judgment.[246] On appeal, the Ninth Circuit wrote:

> The district court did not abuse its discretion by denying Joshua Shapiro's second motion for leave to amend his complaint. Shapiro provided no explanation for why he did not include the additional allegations in his earlier pleadings, and the court properly found that

permitting him to amend his complaint at that point in the litigation would prejudice the defendants. . . .

Shapiro also challenges the district court's grant of summary judgment to the defendants on his claims for discrimination, retaliation, breach of contract, breach of the implied covenant of good faith and fair dealing, and negligent infliction of emotional distress. We affirm the grant of summary judgment for the reasons stated in the district court's well-reasoned order. For example, the district court correctly determined that the evidence in the record did not raise a triable issue of material fact as to whether defendants denied Shapiro accommodations for his learning disability. Similarly, the district court appropriately found that Shapiro was not subjected to any retaliatory action by defendants, who neither failed to provide the necessary documents to support Shapiro's [Public Interest] scholarship application [to the California Bar Foundation] nor denied Shapiro access to Westlaw.[247]

In *Mucci v. Rutgers, the State University of New Jersey School of Law Camden*,[248] Ria L. Mucci was expelled at the end of her third year with a 1.580 GPA.[249] After her sixth readmission petition was denied, she sued the school for breach of contract, disability discrimination (due to its alleged failure to accommodate her "adjustment disorder with anxious features"), and due process violations.[250] In granting the school's motion for summary judgment, the court wrote in pertinent part: "Plaintiff's ADA and [state disability] claims fail because she does not present any evidence suggesting that Rutgers failed to offer her a reasonable accommodation based on the information she provided."[251] The court rejected Mucci's other claims after finding that they too were unsupported (or time-barred).[252]

In *Patton v. Phoenix School of Law LLC*,[253] Angela Patton was expelled after her third semester because she did not have a 2.0 GPA.[254] To gain readmission, Patton sought a TRO in state court.[255] When her request was denied,[256] she sued the school in federal court for disability discrimination (due to her recently diagnosed ADHD) and moved for a preliminary injunction and various other forms of interim relief.[257] In denying all her motions, the court wrote:

> The fact that Plaintiff requested accommodations only after she failed
> to attain the necessary G.P.A. for three semesters in a row—which,
> to Defendant's knowledge, Plaintiff attributed to having to deal with
> the deaths of several family members—and after she was dismissed a
> second time would support a finding of unreasonableness. Plaintiff has
> not demonstrated by a clear showing that she is likely to succeed on
> the merits of her claim that Defendant had a duty to accommodate her
> under these circumstances.[258]

In *Chan v. Board of Regents of Texas Southern University,*[259] Jonathan Chan and Karla Ford were expelled after their first year of law school because each of their GPAs was below 2.0.[260] After their readmission petitions were denied, Chan and Ford sued the school for numerous alleged violations.[261] In granting the school's motion for summary judgment, the court wrote:

> Chan and Ford failed to meet the minimum 2.0 GPA in either first-
> year semester. The basis for the plaintiffs' dismissal was an openly
> announced, objectively academic, and "non-waivable" law school
> policy. (*Id.*) Chan and Ford do not dispute that even before their final
> Contracts II grades, their academic performance was marginal. Their
> attempt to avoid the consequences by asking for a change of their
> Contracts II grades was denied because there was "insufficient evi-
> dence" to support the request. . . . The plaintiffs' contention that their
> "D-" grades [in Contracts II] were "not based upon their performance
> on the examinations" cannot be squared with the undisputed facts. . . .
> The plaintiffs each missed seven of eight multiple-choice questions on
> the final exam, almost 60% of the Contracts II class answered more of
> the multiple-choice questions correctly, and the short-answers and the
> grades were based on the tested material. . . .

Based on the record before this court, the plaintiffs cannot raise a fact dispute as to whether the defendants violated their due-process rights. TSU and [Visiting Professor Shelley] Smith [who taught the Contracts II course] are entitled to summary judgment.[262]

In *Denterlein v. Gamp*,[263] Arti M. Denterlein

> was a law student at San Francisco Law School (SFLS). Shortly before she was scheduled to graduate, she received low grades in two classes, and her grade point average (GPA) for her final year declined. SFLS informed her she was academically disqualified, and she was not allowed to graduate because her fourth-year GPA was too low.[264]

When Denterlein sued,[265] the school filed a demurrer, which was overruled.[266] Subsequently, however, the trial court granted its motion for summary judgment.[267] In affirming this decision, the California Court of Appeal wrote:

> We emphasize again the limited, highly deferential, review we must apply to an action challenging a private university's decision on a student's qualifications for a degree. . . . [W]e may not overturn the decision of a private educational institution regarding a student's qualifications unless "we find it to be arbitrary and capricious, not based upon academic criteria, and the result of irrelevant or discriminatory factors," or "'unless it is such a substantial departure from accepted academic norms as to demonstrate that the person or committee responsible did not actually exercise professional judgment.'" [*Banks v. Dominican College*, 42 Cal. Rptr. 2d 110, 114 (Ct. App. 1995).] While we, like the trial court, are discomfited by the harshness of the result, the record here does not support the findings necessary to overturn SFLS's decision.[268]

In *Cooney v. Barry School of Law*,[269] Joseph Cooney was expelled at the end of his third semester.[270] In response, he asked the school to place him on "discretionary probation" to give him time to bring up his grades.[271] When the school refused, Cooney, who was partially blind, sued it for disability discrimination.[272] Following discovery,[273] the district court granted Barry's motion for summary judgment.[274] On appeal, the Eleventh Circuit, although finding that the district court had committed error, affirmed:

> As an initial matter, we agree with plaintiff that the district court erred in its holding that plaintiff was not disabled. The district court's primary error was its application of the law prior to the 2008 Amendments which modified the definition of the term "disability."
>
> . . . .
>
> The plaintiff mounts two primary arguments supporting his position that the district court also erred in its alternative holdings: first, plaintiff argues that the district court erred in rejecting his claim that Barry violated the ADA when Professor [Elizabeth B.] Megale refused to grant his request for additional time to file his appellate brief in [her] legal writing class; and second, plaintiff argues that the district court erred when it rejected plaintiff's claim of violation when Barry refused to grant his request for extended probation and dismissed him from the school. . . .
>
> Plaintiff's request for additional time was very belated. He approached Professor Megale, at the earliest, shortly before the deadline (i.e., shortly before April 4, 2011), notwithstanding the fact that his eye problem occurred on March 12. . . . [W]e conclude that no reasonable jury could find that plaintiff's belated request for additional time to turn in his brief was a reasonable request for accommodation that would not cause a substantial alteration of the legal writing program. . . . Accordingly, with respect to this first argument of plaintiff, we

cannot conclude that the district court's alternate holding rejecting the argument was erroneous. . . .

[I]n its [second] alternative holding, the district court held that plaintiff was not "otherwise qualified" and therefore rejected plaintiff's challenge. The plaintiff argues on appeal that, if Barry violated the law when Professor Megale refused to grant plaintiff's request for additional time for the brief, then the Committee's reliance on plaintiff's poor grade for that Spring 2011 semester was also a violation. . . .

[B]ecause we have already held that there was no violation when Professor Megale declined to allow an extended briefing deadline, the predicate underlying plaintiff's argument falls away. . . . We [therefore] cannot conclude that the district court erred in . . . rejecting plaintiff's argument challenging the decision to deny extended probation and the consequent dismissal from the school.[275]

In *Banga v. Kanios*,[276] Navjeet S. Banga, a student at the John F. Kennedy School of Law,[277] was expelled for poor grades following his first year of law school.[278] Seeking to be reinstated, Banga sued, claiming that his poor performance was due to a medical disability (anxiety and depression) that the school had failed to properly accommodate.[279]

Banga's first amended complaint was dismissed without prejudice,[280] as was his second amended complaint.[281] Although portions of his third amended complaint were dismissed with prejudice, several of his claims survived.[282] These claims, which accuse the school of breach of contract, disability discrimination, and unfair business practices, remain pending as of this writing due to the parties' extensive motion practice.[283]

In *Gokool v. Oklahoma City University*,[284] Susan R. Gokool was expelled after her first year of law school for poor grades.[285] When her efforts to be reinstated failed, she filed a federal lawsuit against the school.[286] Finding none of her allegations to be colorable, the district court granted the school's motion to dismiss.[287] On appeal, the Tenth Circuit affirmed:

Even though Gokool . . . never disputed her grade point average was below the required minimum, she sued, alleging eight claims for relief: (1) breach of implied contract; (2) bad faith; (3) breach of the duty of good faith and fair dealing; (4) fraud; (5) negligence; (6) conspiracy; (7) disparate treatment; and (8) unjust enrichment. We agree with the district court that none of the claims state plausible claims for relief.[288]

In *Texas Southern University v. Villarreal*,[289] Ivan Villarreal was expelled after his first year of law school with a 1.976 GPA.[290] When his second readmission petition was denied,[291] Villarreal sued the school.[292] It successfully moved to have the case dismissed due to sovereign immunity,[293] but the appeals court reversed and remanded to give Villarreal a chance to pursue his due process claims.[294] The Texas Supreme Court found this to be error:

> Here, Villarreal undisputedly had notice that the School's Rules and Regulations required him to maintain a 2.0 grade point average to continue. And he was given multiple opportunities to appeal his grade and, ultimately, his dismissal. The dean advised students of the opportunity to contest their criminal law grades individually. Villarreal failed to do so. He proceeded to file multiple, admittedly late petitions with the Academic Standards Committee. The committee reviewed and denied his first petition. Villarreal then met with the committee and the dean after filing his second petition, which was later denied. And he was afforded the opportunity to re-enroll after a two-year waiting period. We conclude as a matter of law, therefore, that Villarreal received adequate procedural due course of law in connection with his dismissal.
>
> Turning to substantive due course of law, Villarreal contends that the Student Rules and Regulations and the money he spent on tuition confer a property right to continued graduate education that the Texas Constitution protects against arbitrary or capricious

deprivation. Because our Constitution does not recognize higher education as a fundamental right, however, Villarreal's alleged property right does not fall within any substantive protection provided by the due course of law clause.[295]

In *Daniel v. Brooklyn Law School*,[296] Maurice Daniel was expelled after he failed two courses.[297] Daniel subsequently asked the school "to change [his] grades . . . from 'F' to 'W' and . . . issue a letter stating that his dismissal . . . was the result of missing two final exams due to illness rather than a lack of capacity to complete a course of legal study."[298] When the school refused his requests, Daniel filed a lawsuit in state court, which was dismissed.[299] In affirming this decision, the New York Appellate Division wrote:

> Pursuant to BLS's policy, since the petitioner failed to take two final
> exams, failed to promptly notify the Registrar that he was unable to
> take those exams due to illness, and failed to submit medical documen-
> tation of his illness necessary to schedule make-up exams, he received a
> failing grade in each course. BLS's determination to let the petitioner's
> failing grades stand and to refuse to allow him to withdraw from
> those courses so as to avoid the failing grades was not arbitrary and
> capricious, irrational, made in bad faith, or contrary to constitution or
> statute. . . .[300]

In *Vartanian v. State Bar of California*,[301] the Northwestern California University School of Law[302] expelled Michael H. Vartanian, a third-year student, for poor grades.[303] In response, Vartanian sued both the school and the California Bar, claiming they had worked together to expel him after he complained about a proposed change to the state's ethics rules.[304] Finding that Vartanian had failed to "alleg[e] any facts that would make [his claims] plausible,"[305] the district court dismissed Vartanian's lawsuit.[306] On appeal, the Ninth Circuit affirmed:

[V]artanian could not reasonably have believed that a proposed rule, which involved routine regulation of attorney-client relations and permitted protective actions to be taken on behalf of disabled clients, constituted a violation of the ADA. . . . Also, Vartanian has not alleged enough facts to make plausible his causation claim that the Law School dismissed him . . . at the direction of the State Bar, in retaliation for his letters opposing the proposed rule. . . .[307]

In *Richter v. Catholic University of America*,[308] Brendan Richter was expelled at the end of his first year because his GPA (1.865) was below the law school's required minimum GPA (2.5).[309] In dismissing his lawsuit for breach of contract and lack of good faith and fair dealing, the district court wrote: "The facts in the Amended Complaint are 'not nearly enough to establish evidence from which a fact finder could conclude that there was no rational basis for [CUA Law's] decision' to dismiss Richter."[310]

Lastly, in *Brown v. Suffolk University*,[311] Louis M. Brown was expelled after his first semester of law school because two of his four grades were below a "C."[312] When his readmission petition was denied,[313] Brown sued the school.[314] In granting its motion to dismiss, the court ruled that three of Brown's five claims (breach of contract, disability discrimination, and negligent infliction of emotional distress) failed as a matter of law because Brown never advised the school he needed to use a laptop in class,[315] while the other two (intentional infliction of emotional distress and tortious interference) were not plausible.[316]

1   *See* Joshua M. Silverstein, *A Case for Grade Inflation in Legal Educa-
    tion*, 47 U.S.F. L. REV. 487, 497-98 (2013). As Silverstein points out,
    law schools are an anomaly—most graduate programs require stu-
    dents to maintain a 3.0, or "B," average. *Id.* at 490.

2   478 F.2d 1137 (2d Cir. 1973).

3   *Id.* at 1139-40. At the time of their expulsions, Grafton had a 3.02
    GPA (out of a possible 5.0) and Silversmith had a 2.97 GPA. *See Oust-
    ed Law Students Seek 12M Day in Court*, DAILY NEWS (NY), Feb. 15,
    1972, at 27.

4   *Grafton*, 478 F.2d at 1139-40.

5   *Id.* at 1138. *See also Charles Wender, Grafton Suit Fails*, JUSTINIAN,
    Dec. 20, 1972, at 1, *available at* https://brooklynworks.brooklaw.
    edu/cgi/viewcontent.cgi?article=1065&context=justinian.

6   *Grafton*, 478 F.2d at 1140. Years later, the *Justinian* wrote about the
    case and provided an update:

> The lead story in the February 18, 1972 issue concerned a lawsuit
> brought against BLS by expelled students, Sam Grafton and Lyle
> Silversmith. The stated reason for expulsion by BLS was, "failure
> to maintain the minimum required scholastic average." Plaintiffs
> argued that the minimum standard was arbitrary and capricious.
> They also argued that they were being discriminated against for
> publishing controversial articles in **Justinian**. Both were contribu-
> tors to the paper. While neither was reinstated into the law school,
> one was permitted to take the Bar Examination after fulfilling a
> service requirement with a law firm. He passed and is now a prac-
> ticing attorney.

Joel Mitofsky, *History from the JUSTINIAN Files*, JUSTINIAN, Mar. 29, 1977, at 6, 8 (bold in original), *available at* https://brooklynworks. brooklaw.edu/cgi/viewcontent.cgi?article=1100&context=justini an. In fact, both Grafton and Silversmith were admitted to the New York bar in 1974. *See Samuel Grafton*, LINKEDIN, *at* https://www. linkedin.com/in/samuel-grafton-3b256518/ (last visited Apr. 1, 2022) (indicating that Grafton is a partner in the New York City law firm of Popper & Grafton); *Lyle Silversmith*, LINKEDIN, *at* https://www. linkedin.com/in/lyle-silversmith-2a21237/ (last visited Apr. 1, 2022) (indicating that Silversmith works as a "Per Diem Attorney at New York State Supreme Court").

7   258 N.W.2d 108 (Minn. 1977).

8   *Id.* at 110.

9   *Id.*

10 *Id.* For the details of MSL's merger with Hamline, see Terry Andrews, *Hamline University School of Law: A History of Its First Ten Years* 11-15 (1984), *available at* http://www.minnesotalegalhistory-project.org/assets/Hamline%20Law%20School%20History.pdf.

11 *Abbariao*, 258 N.W.2d at 110.

12 *Id.*

13 *Id.*

14 *Id.* at 111.

15 *Id.* at 112. Unwilling to keep fighting, Abbariao switched gears and opened a medical staffing business called Midwest Clinic Management, Inc. *See Display Ad*, DAILY TIMES (St. Cloud, MN), Aug. 14, 1978, at 6. *See also* Scott Smith, *Filipino Nurses Ease Shortage*, MINNEAPOLIS/ST. PAUL BUS. J., May 19, 2002, *available at* https://www. bizjournals.com/twincities/stories/2002/05/20/story5.html (describing Abbariao as a "retired health-care consultant").

16 571 P.2d 798 (Mont. 1977).

17 *Id.* at 799. As the court explains, this was Johnson's second expulsion:

> Plaintiff entered the University of Montana School of Law in the fall of 1973, and successfully completed her first two semesters of study. She received a grade of F in the Constitutional Law course and grades of D in two other courses taken during her third semester, and consequently, was deficient by eleven grade points at the end of that semester. Plaintiff was excluded from the law school under the applicable exclusionary rule which provides that students with a deficiency of six or more grade points at the end of their third semester are not allowed to continue their law studies. Plaintiff's second petition for readmission subsequent to that exclusion was granted by the law school faculty, and she returned for the next academic year. At the end of that year, her academic performance was deficient by eight grade points. Plaintiff was excluded again, in this instance for failure to meet the law school requirement that a student have a cumulative grade point average of 2.0, which is a zero grade point deficiency, at the completion of the fourth semester.

Id.

18 *Id.* at 798-99.

19 *Id.* at 802-03. Following her expulsion, Johnson became a real estate agent. *See Association of Realtors Elects New Butte Officers,* MONTANA STANDARD (Butte), Oct. 7, 1979, at 27 (reporting on Johnson's election as vice president of the Butte chapter of the Montana Association of Relators). *See also Happy to Be Rescued,* MONTANA STANDARD (Butte), Dec. 7, 2009, at A2 (letter by Johnson thanking her rescuers after she got "stuck on a drifted mountain road" while "accompany[ing] prospective buyers to acreage in the Mount Haggin area.").

20 156 Cal. Rptr. 190 (Ct. App.), *rev'd,* 602 P.2d 778 (Cal. 1979) (in bank).

21 *Id.* at 779. At the time of his expulsion, Paulsen's GPA was 1.92. *See Paulsen*, 156 Cal. Rptr. at 191.

22 *Paulsen*, 602 P.2d at 780.

23 *See Paulsen*, 156 Cal. Rptr. at 190.

24 *Paulsen*, 602 P.2d at 782.

25 431 N.Y.S.2d 60 (App. Div. 1980).

26 *Id.* at 61-62. The opinion does not give Shields's GPA.

27 *Id.* at 61.

28 *Id.* at 63. After losing her lawsuit, Shields read law, got admitted to the New York bar, and then moved to St. Croix, where she had a long career working as a U.S.V.I. assistant attorney general and, in her spare time, starting an art museum. *See Candia Atwater-Shields*, LinkedIn, *at* https://www.linkedin.com/in/candia-atwater-shields-0858455/ (last visited Apr. 1, 2022). *See also Candia Atwater-Shields Inducted into Cambridge Who's Who*, 24-7 Press Release, Dec. 29, 2011, *at* https://www.24-7pressrelease.com/press-release/254798/candia-at-water-shields-inducted-into-cambridge-whos-who.

29 618 P.2d 106 (Wash. Ct. App. 1980), *review denied*, 95 Wash. 2d 1002 (1981).

30 *Id.* at 107-08. The court does not give Maas's GPA.

31 *Id.* As the court explains, "The University of Washington accepted Maas, despite her not being in good academic standing, either by mistake or because good standing is not a prerequisite to admission to their summer program." *Id.* at 108 n.1.

32 *Id.* at 107. In her lawsuit, Maas, who had applied to law school when she was almost fifty, insisted that Gonzaga knew that she was bound to fail because her undergraduate GPA (earned nearly thirty years earlier at Brooklyn College) was 1.84 and her score on the Law School Admission Test was 438 (out of a possible 800). Maas also insisted she would not have left her tenured teaching job in Juneau, Alaska (where she was earning $19,950 a year) if Gonzaga had made

it clear to her that her prospects for success were bleak. *See id.* (further explaining that Maas "attended Gonzaga with the assistance of the Western Interstate Commission for Higher Education . . . which enabled the State of Alaska to substantially pay for her law school tuition."). *See also 'False Hopes': Ex-Student Suing School,* SPOKANE DAILY CHRON., Aug. 24, 1978, at 5.

33 *Maas,* 618 P.2d at 110. For a further look at the case, see *Gonzaga Not Required to 'Warn the Obvious,'* SPOKANE DAILY CHRON., Oct. 16, 1980, at 3 (Metro). Maas subsequently returned to Juneau and became an advocate for persons with developmental disabilities. *See PACS to Meet,* DAILY SITKA SENTINEL (AK), Jan. 20, 1983, at 6.

34 648 P.2d 94 (Wash. Ct. App.), *review denied,* 97 Wash. 2d 1037 (1982), *cert. denied,* 460 U.S. 1013 (1983).

35 *Id.* at 95.

36 *Id.*

37 *Id.*

38 *Id.* at 96.

39 *Id.* at 98-99. *See also Law School Vindicated,* OLYMPIAN (Olympia, WA), May 18, 1982, at A7 (reporting that after the court's ruling, Marquez was "reached in Sunnyside by Yakima radio station KIMA [and] said he was not surprised by the appeals court decision. . . .").

40 719 F.2d 69 (4th Cir. 1983).

41 *Id.* at 70-71.

42 As the court explains, while serving as the "president of the national Association of Student International Law Societies (ASILS), in Washington, D.C.[,] [Henson] was charged by fellow University of Virginia students with removing a moot court problem from national headquarters[.]" *Id.* at 70. Although the Honor Committee twice found Henson guilty, both convictions were overturned, at which point "[t]he students bringing the charges . . . withdrew the

allegations in January, 1981, terminating [the] Honor Committee proceedings." *Id.* at 71.

43   *Id.* at 70.

44   *Id.* at 71-72.

45   *Id.* at 72. By the time the Fourth Circuit ruled, Henson had taken, and passed, the Virginia bar exam. *See Plans Appeal of Conviction*, LEADER (Staunton, VA), Nov. 20, 1978, at 7. As one might expect, Henson's current biography glosses over his law school struggles and confusingly reports that he did graduate. *See Josiah D. Henson*, IPO PANG XINGPU, *at* https://ipopang.com/team/josiah-d-henson/ (last visited Apr. 1, 2022) ("Josiah D. Henson is [a] Senior Partner at IPO Pang Xingpu Law Firm. . . . Mr. Henson is a graduate of Harvard University and the University of Virginia School of Law and is a member of the DC and Virginia Bars.").

46   Civ. A. No. 86-4352, 1986 WL 11472 (E.D. Pa. Oct. 10, 1986), *aff'd on reconsideration*, Civ. A. No. 86-4352, 1987 WL 6747 (E.D. Pa. Feb. 13, 1987), *aff'd mem.*, 833 F.2d 303 (3d Cir. 1987).

47   *Chezik*, 1986 WL 11472, at *1.

48   *Id.*

49   *Id.* at *2.

50   *Id.* Chezik subsequently filed a new federal lawsuit against the school contending that he had found evidence that proved it had tampered with his grades. *See* Dan Orr, *Expelled Law Student Sues School*, SCRANTONIAN (Scranton, PA), June 21, 1987, at B9 (reporting that Chezik now insisted his GPA was 3.16). *See also Clarify Chezik School Lawsuit*, SCRANTONIAN (Scranton, PA), July 5, 1987, at A14. It is not known what happened to this lawsuit.

51   665 F. Supp. 1372 (W.D. Wis. 1987), *aff'd*, 841 F.2d 737 (7th Cir. 1988).

52   *Id.* at 739.

53   *Id.*

54   *Id.*

55 *Id.* at 739-41. For a further look at the case, see Elizabeth R. Smith, Comment, *Anderson v. University of Wisconsin: Handicap and Race Discrimination in Readmission Procedures*, 15 J.C. & U.L. 431 (1989).

Shortly after losing his appeal, Anderson was accused of welfare fraud. *See Man, 44, Charged with Welfare Fraud*, Capital Times (Madison, WI), Aug. 10, 1990, at 4A (reporting that Anderson, who by this time was homeless, also had outstanding warrants for battery and disorderly conduct). *See also On the Record*, Capital Times (Madison, WI), May 17, 1997, at 3A (reporting on Anderson's recent conviction for drunk driving). In 2001, Anderson, still living near the law school, passed away. *See Fradus Lee Anderson in the Wisconsin, U.S., Death Records, 1959-2004, available at* https://www.ancestry.com/discoveryui-content/view/1817748:61483.

56 544 N.Y.S.2d 829 (App. Div.), *appeal granted*, 546 N.Y.S.2d 543 (App. Div. 1989), *order aff'd as modified*, 556 N.E.2d 1104 (N.Y. 1990).

57 Keane's identity was masked throughout her first lawsuit. Her real name was used in her second lawsuit. *See infra* note 62 of this chapter.

58 *See Susan M.*, 556 N.E. at 1105.

59 *Id.*

60 *Id.* at 1106.

61 *Susan "M,"* 544 N.Y.S.2d at 832.

62 *Susan M.*, 556 N.E. at 1107-08. Keane subsequently brought a second lawsuit against the school. Finding it to be a redux of her first lawsuit, both the trial court and the appellate division ruled that it was barred by *res judicata. See* Keane v. New York L. Sch., 589 N.Y.S.2d 18, 19 (App. Div. 1992).

Keane's lawsuits inspired Robert Rains, a professor at Dickinson Law School, to pen two poems. *See* Robert E. Rains, *The Cautionary Ballad of Susan M.*, 40 J. Legal Educ. 485 (1990), and Robert E. Rains, *Susan M. Reprised*, 43 J. Legal Educ. 149 (1993). For a more serious look at the case, see Harold Weinberger & Andrew Schepard, *Judicial Review of Academic Student Evaluations: A Comment on Susan "M" v. New York Law School from Those Who Litigated It*, 77 WEST'S EDUC. L. REP. 1089 (1992) (article written by the school's lawyers).

63 562 A.2d 570 (Conn. Ct. App.), *certification denied*, 567 A.2d 832 (Conn. 1989).

In 1992, the law school became part of Quinnipiac University. *See* Katherine Farrish, *Quinnipiac Takes Over UB Law School*, HARTFORD COURANT, Mar. 3, 1992, at B1. As has been explained elsewhere:

> [When the] University of Bridgeport went through financial hardships in the early 1990s[, it decided to accept] financial assistance from the Professors World Peace Academy, . . . an organization affiliated with [South Korea's] Reverend Sun Myung Moon. The law school decided that Rev. Moon was an unworthy associate and severed any legal relations with the University. In order for the law school to remain open it had to merge with a financially sound university. The law school received bids to be taken over by nearby Sacred Heart University, Fairfield University, and Quinnipiac University. The law school faculty and students voted to merge with Quinnipiac University because they felt it was . . . more financially sound . . . than Sacred Heart.

Quinnipiac University School of Law, LEARN AND GET IT, June 2015, *at* http://learn-and-get-it.blogspot.com/2015/06/quinnipiac-university-school-of-law.html (last visited Apr. 1, 2022).

64 *Gold*, 562 A.2d at 571.

65 *Id.* The school quickly made it known that it took issue with all of Gold's allegations:

> A suit has been filed against the University of Bridgeport Law School by a former student who says he was flunked intentionally by officials intent on impressing the American Bar Association.

Glenn M. Gold, 24, of West Hartford claims the 5-year-old school wanted to show the ABA it was academically tough and deserved national accreditation by giving him arbitrary grades.

The law school received provisional accreditation from the bar association in 1979 and is waiting for a decision on final ABA approval.

Dean Howard [A.] Glickstein denied the school's grading system was unfair. He attributed the suit and others like it to a perception that Bridgeport is "more vulnerable" to student litigation than more established schools.

"If you're going to run an institution of any quality, you have to have standards," Glickstein said Wednesday.

Previous suits against the school have failed and Glickstein said he was confident Gold's would be unsuccessful.

He said the case was "very, very heart-rending," but added that students often become "desperate when they flunk out and try to do anything to get back in."

. . . .

Gold, a first-year student in 1980-81, received two D grades he didn't deserve, said attorney Irving Pinsky. The grades made Gold unable to maintain the required C average, he said.

Ex-Student Sues Bridgeport School, MANCHESTER HERALD (CT), May 6, 1982, at 4.

66 Gold, 562 A.2d at 571.

67 Id. at 573.

68 883 F.2d 1481 (9th Cir.), mandate clarified, 892 F.2d 51 (9th Cir. 1989), appeal after remand, 930 F.2d 29 (table), No. 90-55572, 1991 WL 43314 (9th Cir. Mar. 29, 1991).

69 The University of West Los Angeles, a non-ABA-approved law school, is an accredited California law school (meaning that its graduates can sit for the California bar exam). *See* University of West Los Angeles, *Accreditation, at* https://www.uwla.edu/apps/pages/index.jsp?uREC_ID=321729&type=d (last visited Apr. 1, 2022).

70 *Radcliff*, 1991 WL 43314, at *1.

71 *See Radcliff*, 883 F.2d at 1482.

72 *Radcliff*, 1991 WL 43314, at *1.

73 *See Radcliff*, 883 F.2d at 1482.

74 *Id.* at 1483.

75 *See Radcliff*, 1991 WL 43314, at *1.

76 *Id.*

77 908 F.2d 967 (table), No. 90-2612, 1990 WL 101652 (4th Cir. June 20, 1990), *later proceedings at* Civ. A. No. 3:89-2150-OB, 1992 WL 501791 (D.S.C. Sept. 30, 1992), *aff'd mem.*, 986 F.2d 1414 (table), No. 92-2405, 1993 WL 36114 (4th Cir.), *cert. denied*, 510 U.S. 881 (1993).

78 *Nolan*, 1992 WL 501791, at *3.

79 *Id.* at *1.

80 *Id.* at *3.

81 *Nolan*, 1993 WL 36114, at *1.

82 Civ. A. No. 91-4328, 1992 WL 189489 (E.D. La. July 24, 1992), *aff'd*, 3 F.3d 850 (5th Cir. 1993), *cert. denied*, 510 U.S. 1131 (1994).

83 *Id.* at 854.

84 According to the district court, "Plaintiff injured his head and spine in an automobile accident in 1968. He suffered two additional head injuries in 1972, and fractured his spine in 1979. His injuries have required and continue to require extensive treatment and a number of surgical procedures." *McGregor*, 1992 WL 189489, at *1 n.1.

85 *Id.* at *1 ("In his original and two amending complaints, plaintiff asserts causes of action against defendants under section 504 of the

Rehabilitation Act of 1973, 29 U.S.C. § 794; the due process clause of the Fourteenth Amendment; 42 U.S.C. §§ 1983, 1985 and 1988; Louisiana's Civil Rights Act for Handicapped Persons, LSA R.S. § 46:2251–56; and the Americans with Disabilities Act of 1990, 101 Pub.L. 336, 104 Stat. 327.").

86 *Id.* at *7 ("Mr. McGregor's ambition and desire for furthering his education and his willingness to endure significant hardships in his attempt to achieve his goals are commendable. Congress has mandated that schools such as L.S.U. Law School must make reasonable accommodations to eliminate disadvantageous treatment of disabled students such as plaintiff. It is unfortunate that plaintiff's needs are such that the conditions which would have to be imposed upon the law school to meet those needs go beyond what the law requires. His suit must therefore be dismissed.").

87 *McGregor,* 3 F.3d at 860.

88 980 F.2d 730 (table), No. 92-1587, 1992 WL 363609 (6th Cir. Dec. 9, 1992), *cert. denied,* 510 U.S. 834, *reh'g denied,* 510 U.S. 1005 (1993).

89 *Id.* at *1 (describing Johnson as "a failed law student of Detroit College of Law (DCL) who was unable to achieve a '2.0' overall grade point average at the conclusion of the first two regular semesters.").

90 *Id.*

91 *Id.* at *1-2. Many years later, when he did not get a sales job with a medical device company, Johnson sued for age discrimination. In affirming the district court's grant of summary judgment in favor of the company, the Seventh Circuit wrote:

> Johnson is no stranger to federal-court litigation. Fourteen years ago he sued a financial services company for age discrimination after he was turned down for an internship offered to recent college graduates contemplating an MBA; Johnson was approximately twenty years out of college and already had a master's degree. *Johnson v. Prudential Inv. Corp.,* No. 95 C 5513 (N.D. Ill. filed Sept. 26, 1995). Then he sued a temp agency for disability discrimination,

claiming that the agency refused to place him because he is missing a number of teeth. *Johnson v. Am. Chamber of Commerce Publishers, Inc.*, 108 F.3d 818 (7th Cir.1997). When Reader's Digest mentioned that suit in an article about frivolous litigation under the Americans with Disabilities Act, Johnson sued the publisher for defamation. *Johnson v. Readers Digest Assoc., Inc.*, No. 99 C 2920 (N.D. Ill. filed May 3, 1999). Most recently he sued a women's advocacy group for gender discrimination after the organization declined to hire him as a counselor serving female victims of domestic violence. *Johnson v. Apna Ghar, Inc.*, 330 F.3d 999 (7th Cir.2003). Each case ultimately settled. On top of all these, after Johnson flunked out of law school, he sued the school and its faculty under a number of theories. *Johnson v. Detroit Coll. of Law*, 1992 WL 363609 (6th Cir. Dec. 9, 1992) (unpublished opinion).

Johnson v. Cook Inc., 327 F. App'x 661, 663 (7th Cir. 2009), *cert. denied*, 558 U.S. 1155, *reh'g denied*, 559 U.S. 1046 (2010).

92 No. C4-93-2074, 1994 WL 175019 (Minn. Ct. App. May 10, 1994).

93 *Id.* at *2. Robinson's grades caused him to rank last in the freshman class. *Id.*

94 *Id.* at *1.

95 *Id.*

96 *Id.* at *6.

97 27 F.3d 1120 (6th Cir. 1994).

98 *Id.* at 1122-23. Although the court does not say how far below a 2.0 Megenity was at the time of his expulsion, it does quote the school's handbook, which provided:

> Any [day] student whose cumulative grade point average at the end of any semester is 1.6 . . . but less than 2.0 shall be placed on probation for one semester. Except as is provided in Rule (1), any student on probation who does not remove all grade point

deficiency in the next semester in which enrolled, shall be dismissed from the School of Law.

Id. at 1122.

99 *Id.* at 1122-23.

100 *Id.* at 1122.

101 *Id.*

102 *Id.* at 1125.

103 *Id.*

104 617 N.Y.S.2d 825 (App. Div. 1994).

105 *Id.* at 826. The court's opinion does not provide any further details about Sage's expulsion.

106 *Id.*

107 *Id.*

108 882 F. Supp. 1176 (D.N.H. 1994), *aff'd*, 56 F.3d 59 (table), No. 95-1003, 1995 WL 325791 (1st Cir. May 31, 1995). In 2010, Franklin Pierce Law Center became part of the University of New Hampshire. *See UNH, Law Center Merger Complete*, BURLINGTON FREE PRESS (VT), Aug. 31, 2010, at 5B (reporting that the law school "is officially being renamed the University of New Hampshire School of Law.").

109 *Murphy*, 882 F. Supp. at 1178-80. Although the court does not recite Murphy's complete transcript, it does quote a faculty report that found a "pattern" to Murphy's grades. While she had earned "As" and "Bs" in her experiential courses, she had gotten "Cs, Ds, and Fs" in her doctrinal courses. *See id.* at 1179-80.

110 *Id.* at 1177.

111 *Id.* at 1181.

112 *Id.* at 1183.

113 *Murphy*, 1995 WL 325791, at *5.

114 621 N.Y.S.2d 85 (App. Div. 1994).

115 *Id.* at 85. The court's opinion does not say how far Girsky was from a 2.0.

116 *Id.* at 86.

117 *Id.*

118 No. Civ. A. 94-5066, 1995 WL 263547 (E.D. Pa. May 2, 1995), *later proceedings at* No. Civ. A. 94-5066, 1995 WL 447588 (E.D. Pa. July 28, 1995), *and later proceedings at* No. Civ. A. 94-5066, 1996 WL 377143 (E.D. Pa. July 2, 1996).

119 *Kunkel,* 1996 WL 377143, at *1.

120 *Id.*

121 *See Kunkel,* 1995 WL 263547, at *1.

122 *See Kunkel,* 1995 WL 447588, at *1.

123 *Kunkel,* 1996 WL 377143, at *2.

124 899 F. Supp. 850 (D.N.H. 1995).

125 *Id.* at 851, 854.

126 *Id.* at 851.

127 *Id.* at 856. Gill's breach of contract and defamation claims similarly were rejected. *See id.* at 856-57.

128 53 Cal. Rptr. 2d 1 (Ct. App. 1996).

129 *Id.* at 2 (explaining that Perez was expelled after his first year because his GPA was 1.731 and after his second year because his GPA was 1.96).

130 *Id.*

131 *Id.* at 2-4.

132 112 F.3d 517 (table), No. 96-56088, 1997 WL 207599 (9th Cir. Apr. 25, 1997), *cert. denied,* 522 U.S. 1050 (1998).

Scott entered Western State University ("WSU") in 1992. *See* Defendant/Appellee's Brief, Scott v. Western St. Univ. Coll. of L., No. 96-56088 (9th Cir. filed Oct. 31, 1996), *available at* 1996 WL 33470172, at *2. At that time, the school, which was founded in 1966, had three campuses (in Fullerton, Irvine, and San Diego); was accredited by the California state bar; and catered mainly (70%) to part-time students. *See* Eric Lichtblau, *Western State Law Campus Will Open*, L.A. TIMES, July 12, 1990, at B2. The court does not mention which campus Scott attended; it also does not indicate if he was a full-time or part-time student. Today, after numerous changes, WSU has a different owner (Westcliff University, a for-profit on-line school); a slightly altered name ("Western State College"); just one campus (which is located not far from its former home in Irvine); is ABA approved; and caters mainly (80%) to full-time students. *See* Allen K. Easley, *What a Ride It Has Been: The Law School That Refused to Quit*, ORANGE CNTY. LAW., Oct. 2019, at 61; *509 Reports, supra* note 3 of Chapter 1 (under "Western State College of Law").

133 *Scott*, 1997 WL 207599, at *1. Scott's GPA at the time of his dismissal was 1.89. *See* Defendant/Appellee's Brief, *supra* note 132 of this chapter, at *2.

134 *See Scott*, 1997 WL 207599, at *1.

135 *Id.* at *1-2.

136 125 F.3d 541 (7th Cir. 1997).

137 The court does not indicate when Waller was expelled nor does it give his GPA. However, the school's appellate brief states that Waller was dismissed at the end of his first year with a 1.645 GPA. *See* Brief of Appellees Board of Trustees of Southern Illinois University et al., Waller v. Southern Ill. Univ., No. 97-1363, at 4 (7th Cir. filed Apr. 29, 1997) [hereinafter BOT Brief], *available at* https://books.google.com/books?id=D-Oz9tN84LEC&pg=PT4&lpg=PT4&dq#v=onepage&q&f=false.

138 *Waller*, 125 F.3d at 541. The school's rule required students to have at least a 1.900 GPA to petition for readmission. *See* BOT Brief, *supra* note 137 of this chapter, at 3.

139 *Waller*, 125 F.3d at 541.

140 *Id.* at 542.

141 No. CJ-99-3712-66, 1999 WL 34987987 (Okla. Dist. Ct. Sept. 7, 1999), *aff'd,* 6 P.3d 509 (Okla. Ct. Civ. App. 2000).

142 *Id.* at 511. No information about Bittle's grades has been located.

143 *Id.* at 511-12. Although Cantrell is not mentioned by name in the court's opinion, he is identified in Bittle's complaint. *See* Bittle v. Oklahoma City Univ., No. CJ-99-3712-66 (Okla Dist. Ct.) (petition dated May 24, 1999), *available at* 1999 WL 33970310, at ¶¶ 8, 16.

144 *Bittle,* 1999 WL 34987987 (star paging unavailable).

145 *Bittle,* 6 P.3d at 515-16.

146 209 F. Supp. 2d 55 (D.D.C. 2002).

147 *Id.* at 57-58. This was not Allison's first brush with disaster. During his first semester of law school, he had received three "Ds." *Id.* at 57. Then, at the end of his second semester, he was given an "F" in his year-long Legal Reasoning, Research, and Writing course. *Id.*

148 *Id.* at 56, 58.

149 *Id.* at 59-60.

150 *Id.* at 60-61.

151 *See id.* at 61-62 (negligence); 62 (improper state action); 62-63 (disability discrimination).

152 No. 323310, 2002 WL 34113228 (Cal. Super. Ct. Sept. 3, 2002), *later proceedings at* No. 323310, 2002 WL 34113230 (Cal. Super. Ct. Oct. 21, 2002), *and later proceedings at* No. A097304, 2002 WL 31439753 (Cal. Ct. App. Oct. 31, 2002), *and judgment entered,* No. 323310, 2002 WL 34113229 (Cal. Super. Ct. Nov. 22, 2002).

153 *Rosenberg,* 2002 WL 31439753, at *1.

154 *Id.*

155 *Id.*

156 *Id.*

157 *Id.*

158 *Id.* at *6.

159 *Rosenberg*, 2002 WL 34113230 (star paging unavailable). In a subsequent order, Rosenberg was directed to pay the school's costs. *See Rosenberg*, 2002 WL 34113229 (star paging unavailable).

160 No. Civ.A. 01-12199DPW, 2003 WL 22914304 (D. Mass. Dec. 9, 2003), *aff'd*, 124 F. App'x 15 (1st Cir. 2005).

161 *Marlon*, 2003 WL 22914304, at *1-3. At the time of her first expulsion, Marlon had a 66.9 GPA but the school required students to have at least a 70.0 GPA. *Id.* at *1 n.4. At the time of her second expulsion, it appears Marlon had a 67.6 GPA. *Id.* at *3 n.11 (my calculation—the court does not give Marlon's actual GPA).

162 *Id.* at *4.

163 *Id.* at *1.

164 *Marlon*, 124 F. App'x at 16. By the time of her lawsuit, Marlon had left Massachusetts. *See Marlon*, 2003 WL 22914304, at *4. Settling in Las Vegas, she became a licensed clinical social worker. *See Ms. Dianne S Marlon LCSW NPI 1649548645*, NPI PROFILE, *at* https://npiprofile.com/npi/1649548645 (last visited Apr. 1, 2022).

165 17 Cal. Rptr. 3d 39 (Ct. App. 2004).

166 *Id.* at 47-48.

167 *Id.* at 48.

168 Chapman opened its law school in 1995 and received provisional ABA approval in 1999. *Id.* at 44-45. Goehring was expelled in January 1998. *Id.* at 45.

169 *Id.*

170 *Id.*

171 *Id.* at 46.

172 *Id.* at 48. (footnote omitted).

173 No. 14-04-01075-CV, 2005 WL 240431 (Tex. Ct. App. Feb. 3, 2005), *later proceedings at* No. 2004-45694, 2006 WL 3480252 (Tex. Dist. Ct. Feb. 28, 2006), *aff'd sub nom.* Jackson v. Texas S. Univ.–Thurgood Marshall Sch. of L., 231 S.W.3d 437 (Tex. Ct. App. 2007).

174 *Id.* at 438. The court does not indicate how far Jackson was from the school's required minimum GPA.

175 *Id.* The memo made up 49% of the course's grade. *Id.*

176 *Id.* Jackson also sued Kim for getting him into trouble, but the court likewise granted Kim's request for summary judgment. *See Jackson,* 2006 WL 3480252 (star paging unavailable). As a result, Kim was able to graduate on time and has been a lawyer in New York since 2007. *See Jong Woo Kim,* New York State Unified Court System—Attorney Online Services—Search, *at* https://iapps.courts.state. ny.us/attorneyservices/wicket/page?3 (last visited Apr. 1, 2022).

177 *Jackson,* 231 S.W. 3d at 439.

178 *Id.* at 440-41.

179 No. B175169, 2005 WL 1663194 (Cal. Ct. App. July 18, 2005).

180 *Id.* at *1.

181 *Id.* at *2.

182 *Id.* at *1.

183 *Id.*

184 *Id.* at *12.

185 412 F. Supp. 2d 814 (S.D. Ohio 2005).

186 *Id.* at 815. Prior to the end of the semester, Peebles reduced his course load from twelve credits to eight credits. *Id.*

187 *Id.*

188 *Id.* at 815-16.

189 *Id.* at 816.

190 *Id.*

191 *Id.* at 816-18. Peebles did not return to the law school. Instead, he opted to earn a Ph.D. in Rehabilitation from Auburn University. He currently serves as the president and chief executive officer of Accessible Alabama, which helps "communities step up to meet current accessible housing needs and prepare for the future's accelerating demand [for such housing]." *See Eric Peebles,* LINKEDIN, *at* https://www.linkedin.com/in/eric-peebles-abilitiesunlimited/ (last visited Apr. 1, 2022).

192 Civil Action No. 04-cv-11838-PBS, 2005 WL 6489754 (D. Mass. Nov. 10, 2005).

193 *Id.* at *2.

194 *Id.* at *4. The court does not indicate what Kiani's GPA was either before or after she was found guilty of plagiarism.

195 *Id.*

196 *Id.*

197 *Id.* at *5.

198 *Id.* at *11. In particular, the magistrate judge found: 1) there was no proof that the school had failed to follow its disciplinary procedures (negating Kiana's breach-of-contract claim); 2) there likewise was no proof that various unflattering remarks allegedly made by the faculty had influenced the outcome of the disciplinary hearing (negating Kiana's ADA claim); and 3) Kiana's Rehabilitation Act claim was time-barred. *See id.* at *5-11.

199 *Id.* at *1.

200 725 N.W.2d 485 (Mich. Ct. App.), *appeal denied,* 723 N.W.2d 858 (Mich. 2006).

201 *Id.* at 487-88.

202 *Id.* at 488.

203 *Id.*

204 *Id.*

205 *Id.*

206 *Id.* The information regarding these two counts comes from Buck's later federal lawsuit. *See infra* note 208 of this chapter.

207 *Buck,* 725 N.W.2d at 488.

208 *Id.* at 489.

By the time of her appeal, Buck had accumulated 88 of the 90 credits she needed to graduate—she was able to accomplish this feat because the TRO had remained in place throughout the litigation. *See id.* at 488 n.4 (criticizing the trial court for both granting and continuing the TRO). In her final semester, however, Buck again was expelled when her GPA fell to 1.98. Believing nevertheless that she was due her degree, Buck filed a new lawsuit in federal court, which was dismissed based on collateral estoppel and *res judicata.* *See* Buck v. Thomas [M.] Cooley Law School, 615 F. Supp. 2d 632 (W.D. Mich. 2009), *aff'd,* 597 F.3d 812 (6th Cir.), *cert. denied,* 562 U.S. 839 (2010). *See also* Elie Mystal, *Cooley Law Dropout Learns a Lesson in Res Judicata,* ABOVE THE LAW, Mar. 17, 2010, *at* https://abovethelaw.com/2010/03/cooley-law-dropout-learns-a-lesson-in-res-judicata/; "Angel," *Tom M. Cooley Hall of Shame! Go Team . . .,* BUT I DID EVERYTHING RIGHT! BLOG, Sept. 27, 2010, *at* http://butidideverythingrightorsoithought.blogspot.com/2010/09/tom-m-cooley-hall-of-shame-go-team.html.

209 Docket No. 274811, 2007 WL 1695908 (Mich. Ct. App. June 12, 2007), *appeal denied,* 743 N.W.2d 58 (Mich. 2008).

210 The court does not provide any information regarding the basis for Dulemba's expulsion.

211 *Id.*

212 *Id.* at *2.

213 *Id.* at *1.

214 *Id.*

215 *Id.* at *4. When Dulemba appealed to the Michigan Supreme Court, it refused review. *See supra* note 209 of this chapter. Justice Kelly, joined by Justice Weaver, dissented:

> Besides finding support for plaintiff's position in MCR 2.114(C)(2), I find the facts of this case analogous to those in *Kirkaldy v. Rim*[, 734 N.W.2d 201 (Mich. 2007)]. In that case, the plaintiff filed with the court an affidavit of merit that was defective. The Court of Appeals determined that the filing did not toll the period of limitations. This Court unanimously reversed, concluding that the statutory period of limitations was tolled when the complaint and affidavit of merit were filed, regardless of whether the affidavit was defective.

> Similarly, here, plaintiff filed a complaint but failed to sign it. In essence, she filed a defective complaint. But just as a defective affidavit of merit was sufficient in *Kirkaldy*, so too should a defective complaint be sufficient here.

> Because I find support for plaintiff's argument in MCR 2.114(C)(2) and in *Kirkaldy*, I would grant leave to appeal to consider whether we should reverse the Court of Appeals decision on this interesting issue.

Dulemba, 743 N.W.2d at 59-60 (footnotes omitted).

216 Case No. CIV-08-477-R, 2008 WL 11384188 (W.D. Okla. Sept. 22, 2008), *later proceedings at* Case No. CIV-08-477-R, 2009 WL 10690873 (W.D. Okla. Nov. 25, 2009), *and later proceedings at* Case No. CIV-08-477-R, 2010 WL 11570736 (W.D. Okla. Jan. 22, 2010), *and later proceedings at* Case No. CIV-08-477-R, 2010 WL 11570737 (W.D. Okla. Jan. 22, 2010), *aff'd sub nom.* Doe v. Oklahoma City Univ., 406 F. App'x 248 (10th Cir. 2010).

217 *Kodatt*, 2010 WL 11570737, at *1.

218 *Id.* Kodatt suffered from "a number of learning disabilities, including attention deficit hyperactivity disorder ["ADHD"] and dyslexia." *Doe,* 406 F. App'x at 249.

219 *See Kodatt,* 2008 WL 11384188, at *2 (dismissing plaintiff's claims for punitive damages and negligent infliction of emotional distress); *Kodatt,* 2009 WL 10690873, at *2 (partially granting plaintiff's document production requests); *Kodatt,* 2010 WL 11570736, at *3 (denying plaintiff's request for judgment on liability or an "adverse inference" jury instruction for the school's alleged spoilation of evidence).

220 *Kodatt,* 2010 WL 11570737, at *1.

221 *Id.*

222 *Id.*

223 *Id.* at *3. The court also granted the school's request for summary judgment on Kodatt's breach of contract, negligence, and promissory estoppel claims. *See id.* at *4-5.

224 *Doe,* 406 F. App'x at 249.

225 *Id.* at 252.

226 617 F. Supp. 2d 1 (D. Mass. 2009).

227 *Id.* at 3.

228 *Id.*

229 *Id.*

230 *Id.* at 6-7.

231 *Id.* at 5. Brodsky did not pursue his lawsuit and now works as a technology freelancer in Israel. *See Seva Brodsky,* LinkedIn, *at* https://www.linkedin.com/in/seva-brodsky-575101/ (last visited Apr. 1, 2022). In addition to mentioning his electrical engineering degrees, Brodsky's profile includes the following entry: "New England Law | Boston[,] J.D. candidate, Jurisprudence with emphasis on Intellectual Property (patents, etc.)[,] 2003-2006." *Id.*

232 No. 2:09-cv-709, 2009 WL 2913919 (S.D. Ohio Sept. 8, 2009).

233 *Id.* at *1, *3.

234 *Id.* at *3.

235 *Id.*

236 *Id.* at *4, *12. Following the failure of his lawsuit, Oser became a real estate investor in Massillon, Ohio. *See Andrew Oser*, LINKEDIN, *at* https://www.linkedin.com/in/andrewoser/ (last visited Apr. 1, 2022).

237 No. 3:09-cv-0074-HES-TEM, 2010 WL 2028089 (M.D. Fla. Feb. 19, 2010), *later proceedings at* No. 3:09-cv-0074-HES-TEM, 2010 WL 1993062, at *1 (M.D. Fla. Apr. 9, 2010), *aff'd*, 395 F. App'x 669, 2010 WL 3551982 (11th Cir. Sept. 14, 2010).

238 *Meisenhelder*, 2010 WL 2028089, at *1-2. The court does not indicate what Meisenhelder's GPA was at the time of her dismissal.

239 *Id.* According to the court, "The Plaintiff has alleged many 'disabilities', but has consistently maintained, and submitted supporting documentation, that she suffered from migraine headaches, depression, and an eating disorder." *Id.* at *3.

240 *Id.* at *3-4. In a subsequent opinion, the court denied the school's request for attorneys' fees:

> Though Plaintiff ultimately lost her claim that Defendant violated the ADA, this does not necessarily render her argument frivolous, unreasonable or without foundation. Plaintiff introduced evidence of her health problems, her various requests for accommodation, and deposition testimony that Defendant failed to give her meaningful accommodation when it rescheduled multiple exams for the same day and failed to digitally record her classes. Although, taken as a whole, the evidence did not provide enough to defeat Defendant's Motion for Summary Judgment, Plaintiff's belief that she had not received accommodation as required by the ADA was not unreasonable.

Meisenhelder, 2010 WL 1993062, at *1.

241 *Meisenhelder*, 2010 WL 3551982, at *1.

242 CV 10-03177 MMM (FMOx), 2010 WL 11601057 (C.D. Cal. Nov. 29, 2010), *later proceedings at* CV 10-03177 MMM (FMOx), 2011 WL 13272256 (C.D. Cal. May 4, 2011), *and later proceedings at* CV 10-03177 MMM (FMOx), 2012 WL 13075281 (C.D. Cal. May 9, 2012), *and later proceedings at* No. CV 10-03177-JGB (FMOx), 2013 WL 4197098 (C.D. Cal. Aug. 12, 2013), *aff'd*, 648 F. App'x 713 (9th Cir. 2016).

Abraham Lincoln University, a non-ABA-approved law school, is an unaccredited California law school. *See* Abraham Lincoln University, *Accreditation & Registration, at* https://www.alu.edu/about/accreditation/ (last visited Apr. 1, 2022). The consequences of being an unaccredited law school are spelled out *infra* note 243 of this chapter.

243 *Shapiro*, 2013 WL 4197098, at *7. As the court explains:

> As a prerequisite for taking the California Bar Exam, students from unaccredited law schools must pass the First-Year Law School Students' Examination ("FYLSX") at the end of their first year of law school. In conformity with the Guidelines for Unaccredited Law School Rules ("Guidelines"), ALU students who do not pass the First Year Law School Examination within three administrations must be promptly disqualified from a law school's J.D. program.

Id. The FYLSX, better known as the Baby Bar Exam, "is a one-day test given twice a year [in June and October]. It consists of four one-hour essay questions and 100 multiple-choice questions. The exam covers three subjects: Contracts, Criminal Law, and Torts. More than 700 applicants take the exam each year." State Bar of California, *First-Year Law Students' Examination, at* https://www.calbar.ca.gov/admissions/examinations (last visited Apr. 1, 2022).

In December 2021, Kim Kardashian (who is reading law under the tutelage of a San Francisco law firm) reported that she had passed the FYLSX on her fourth try. *See* Debra Cassens Weiss, *Kim Kardashian Says She Finally Passed the 'Baby Bar' Exam After Her*

Apprenticeship Studies, ABA J., Dec. 14, 2021, *at* https://www.aba-journal.com/news/article/kim-kardashian-says-she-finally-passed-the-baby-bar-after-her-apprenticeship-studies. As this source explains, "Usually, those taking the baby bar exam get only three times to pass, but California added an extra try because of the COVID-19 pandemic." *Id.*

244 *Shapiro*, 2013 WL 4197098, at *8. The court does not further describe Shapiro's disability.

245 *See Shapiro*, 2010 WL 11601057 (granting Shapiro's motion for leave to file a First Amended Complaint); *Shapiro*, 2011 WL 13272256 (denying Shapiro's motion for leave to file a Second Amended Complaint); *Shapiro*, 2012 WL 13075281 (denying Shapiro's motion for sanctions).

246 *See Shapiro*, 2013 WL 4197098, at *13.

247 *Shapiro*, 648 F. App'x at 713-14.

248 Civil No. 08-4806 (RBK), 2011 WL 831967 (D.N.J. Mar. 3, 2011). In 2015, Rutgers merged its previously separate Camden and Newark law schools. *See* Jonathan Lai, *Rutgers Law Schools Merging in Fall,* PHILA. INQUIRER, Aug. 10, 2015, at B1.

249 *Mucci*, 2011 WL 831967, at *1.

250 *Id.* at *1, *4-6.

251 *Id.* at *21.

252 *See id.* at *10-20.

253 No. CV-11-0748-PHX-GMS, 2011 WL 1936920 (D. Ariz. May 20, 2011). The Phoenix School of Law opened in 2005, changed its name to Arizona Summit Law School in 2013, and closed in 2018. *See* Anne Ryman, *Arizona Summit Law School Details Closure Plan,* ARIZ. RE-PUBLIC (Phoenix), Oct. 26, 2018, at 18A.

254 *Patton*, 2011 WL 1936920, at *1. This was Patton's second expulsion. She had been expelled after her second semester but let back in on

the condition that she bring her cumulative GPA up to a 2.0. During her third semester, however, she earned a 1.69 GPA. *Id.*

255 *Id.*

256 *Id.* at *2.

257 *Id.* at *1-2. In addition to a preliminary injunction, Patton requested pro bono counsel, expedited handling, permission to file electronically, and an order to show cause. *See id.* at *1.

258 *Id.* at *4.

259 Civil Action No. H-12-0325, 2012 WL 5832494 (S.D. Tex. Nov. 16, 2012).

260 *Id.* at *1 (explaining that Chan had a 1.82 GPA and Ford had a 1.83 GPA).

261 *Id.* Chan and Ford accused the school of breach of contract, negligent hiring, negligent and intentional infliction of severe mental distress, and violation of their due process rights. *Id.*

262 *Id.* at *5-6. Having dismissed Chan and Ford's only federal claim, the court declined to retain their state law claims. *See id.* at *7. For a further look at the case, see Harvey Gilmore, *Law School Grades: Flunked Out, But Did Not Really Fail*, 7 CHARLESTON L. REV. 207 (2012-2013).

263 No. CGC-13-531393, 2013 WL 9853658 (Cal. Super. Ct. Dec. 23, 2013), *later proceedings at* A144516, 2017 WL 6506583 (Cal. Ct. App. Dec. 20, 2017).

264 *Denterlein*, 2017 WL 6506583, at *1. According to the court, Denterlein

> attended SFLS from fall 2005 until spring 2009. During each term until spring 2009, she maintained GPA's above 70. In spring 2009, however, she received a final grade of 64 in her commercial law class and a final grade of 63 in her choice of law class. As a result, her GPA for her fourth year was 67.20. Her cumulative grade point average was 72.76.

> Jane O'Hara Gamp, SFLS's dean, wrote a letter to plaintiff on May 26, 2009, informing her that she had been academically disqualified because her fourth-year GPA was below 70 percent, and that she would not be permitted to graduate during the commencement exercises that were to take place on May 31, 2009.

Id. at *2 (footnote omitted). Although SFLS, a non-ABA-approved law school, has been an accredited California law school since 1937 (meaning that its graduates can sit for the California bar exam), as of January 1, 2022, its accreditation status is in jeopardy due to its low bar pass rate. *See* San Francisco Law School, *Notice of Probationary Status through July 1, 2022, at* https://sfls.edu/ (last visited Apr. 1, 2022) (under "Accreditation").

265 Denterlein's multi-count complaint alleged "breach of contract, unfair trade practices, violation of her constitutional rights, fraud, breach of the implied covenant of good faith and fair dealing, negligence, and declaratory relief. . . ." *Denterlein*, 2017 WL 6506583, at *1.

266 *See Denterlein*, 2013 WL 9853658, at *1.

267 *Denterlein*, 2017 WL 6506583, at *1.

268 *Id.* at *7.

269 Case No: 6:14-cv-106-Orl-22KRS, 2014 WL 12616979 (M.D. Fla. Oct. 30, 2014), *later proceedings at* Case No: 6:14-cv-106-Orl-22KRS, 2015 WL 12835701 (M.D. Fla. Sept. 25, 2015), *and later proceedings at* Case No: 6:14-cv-106-Orl-22KRS, 2015 WL 12835702 (M.D. Fla. Nov. 5, 2015), *and later proceedings at* Case No: 6:14-cv-106-Orl-22KRS, 2016 WL 7130941 (M.D. Fla. Mar. 9, 2016), *aff'd*, 720 F. App'x 571 (11th Cir.), *cert. denied*, 139 S. Ct. 174, *reh'g denied*, 139 S. Ct. 585 (2018).

270 *Cooney*, 2016 WL 7130941, at *1-2.

271 *Id.* at *2. The court does not indicate what Cooney's GPA was at the time of his dismissal.

272 *Id.* at *1. Cooney originally brought his suit in the Eastern District of New York. The case was transferred to the Middle District of Florida

after New York was determined to be an inconvenient forum. *See Cooney*, 2014 WL 12616979, at *1.

273 *See Cooney*, 2015 WL 12835701 (granting school's motion to compel production of documents); *Cooney*, 2015 WL 12835702 (denying Cooney's motion for sanctions for failure to produce information).

274 *See Cooney*, 2016 WL 7130941, at *1.

275 *Cooney*, 720 F. App'x at 572-75.

276 Case No. 16-cv-04270-RS, 2016 WL 7230870 (N.D. Cal. Dec. 14, 2016).

277 The John F. Kennedy School of Law ("JFKSOL"), a non-ABA-approved law school, originally was part of John F. Kennedy University ("JFKU"). In 2021, the law school became part of Northcentral University after JFKU closed. *See Northcentral Takes JFK Law Online*, PreLaw, Spring 2021, at 6. JFKSOL is an accredited California law school (meaning that its graduates can sit for the California bar exam). *See* Northcentral University, *School of Law—Accreditation, at* https://www.ncu.edu/law/accreditation (last visited Apr. 1, 2022).

278 *Banga*, 2016 WL 7230870, at *1. The court does not provide Banga's GPA.

279 *Id.*

280 *Id.* at *6.

281 *See* Banga v. Kanios, Case No. 16-cv-04270-RS, 2017 WL 11637328, at *1 (N.D. Cal. May 11, 2017).

282 *See* Banga v. Kanios, Case No. 16-cv-04270-RS, 2017 WL 6731639, at *1 (N.D. Cal. Dec. 29, 2017).

283 To date, these motions have resulted in fourteen opinions. *See* Banga v. Kanios, Case No. 16-cv-04270-RS, at 2018 WL 11360090 (N.D. Cal. Jan. 16, 2018) (denying plaintiff's motion for a preliminary injunction requiring the law school to re-enroll him immediately); 2018 WL 11360092 (N.D. Cal. Mar. 15, 2018) (same); 2018 WL 11360187 (N.D. Cal. Mar. 20, 2018) (striking certain affirmative defenses); 2019 WL 6905217 (N.D. Cal. Dec. 19, 2019) (discovery requests); 2020 WL

1492694 (N.D. Cal. Mar. 27, 2020) (granting summary judgment to defendants on plaintiff's retaliation claim and partial summary judgment on his breach of contract claim); 2020 WL 1865139 (N.D. Cal. Apr. 13, 2020) (denying plaintiff's motion for contempt); 2020 WL 1905557 (N.D. Cal. Apr. 16, 2020); 2020 WL 10357151 (N.D. Cal. Aug. 14, 2020) (denying defendants' motion for an independent medical examination of the plaintiff); 2020 WL 9037179 (N.D. Cal. Dec. 9, 2020) (denying plaintiff's motion to exclude defendant's medical expert); 2021 WL 1117336 (N.D. Cal. Mar. 24, 2021) (resolving fee dispute involving plaintiff's economic damages expert); 2021 WL 1743540 (N.D. Cal. May 4, 2021) (same); 2021 WL 1941758 (N.D. Cal. May 14, 2021) (same); 2021 WL 2952824 (N.D. Cal. June 25, 2021) (same); and 2021 WL 4133754 (N.D. Cal. Sep. 10, 2021) (rulings on various motions *in limine*).

284 Case No. CIV-16-807-R, 2016 WL 10520949 (W.D. Okla. Dec. 29, 2016), *motion to alter or amend judgment denied*, Case No. CIV-16-807, 2017 WL 5241239 (W.D. Okla. May 1, 2017), *aff'd*, 716 F. App'x 815 (10th Cir. 2017), *and later proceedings at* 770 F. App'x 894 (10th Cir.), *cert. denied*, 140 S. Ct. 490 (2019).

285 Neither the court opinions nor the parties' pleadings reveal Gokool's GPA.

286 *Gokool*, 2016 WL 10520949, at *1-2.

287 *Id.* at *1.

288 *Gokool*, 716 F. App'x at 817. Gokool subsequently sought to disqualify the trial judge for partiality. When her effort failed, Gokool again appealed to the Tenth Circuit. Not only did it affirm, it upheld the trial judge's order barring Gokool from filing any new motions "unless she obtains a licensed attorney who certifies that the motion is non-frivolous." *Gokool*, 770 F. App'x at 898-99.

289 No. 2016-64945, 2017 WL 10939047 (Tex. Dist. Ct. July 10, 2017), *new trial denied*, No. 2016-64945, 2017 WL 10939048 (Tex. Dist. Ct. Oct. 9,

2017), *rev'd and remanded*, 570 S.W.3d 916 (Tex. Ct. App. 2018), *rev'd*, 620 S.W.3d 899 (Tex. 2021).

290 *Villarreal*, 620 S.W.3d at 903.

291 *Id.* at 903-04.

292 *Id.* at 904.

293 *Id.* at 903.

294 *Id.*

295 *Id.* at 909. Despite losing his lawsuit, Villarreal continues to list on his *LinkedIn* page the years he would have been enrolled in the law school (2014-17) and the degree he would have received ("J.D.") if he had graduated. *See Ivan Villarreal*, LINKEDIN, *at* https://www.linkedin.com/in/ivan-villarreal-7a92b375/ (last visited Apr. 1, 2022).

296 60 N.Y.S.3d 308 (App. Div. 2017), *leave to appeal denied*, 95 N.E.3d 324 (N.Y.), *motion for leave to proceed in forma pauperis denied*, 139 S. Ct. 308, *cert. denied*, 139 S. Ct. 478 (2018).

297 *Daniel*, 60 N.Y.S.3d at 309.

298 *Id.*

299 *Id.*

300 *Id.* at 310.

301 Case No. 5:18-cv-00826-EJD, 2018 WL 2724343 (N.D. Cal. June 6, 2018), *reconsideration denied*, Case No. 5:18-cv-00826-EJD, 2018 WL 3609087 (N.D. Cal., July 27, 2018), *aff'd*, 794 F. App'x 597 (9th Cir. 2019), *cert. denied*, 141 S. Ct. 258 (2020).

302 "NWCULaw" (as the school calls itself), a non-ABA-approved law school, is an accredited California law school (meaning that its graduates can sit for the California bar exam). *See* Northwestern California University School of Law, *Accreditation, at* https://nwculaw.edu/accreditation (last visited Apr. 1, 2022).

303 The various court opinions do not provide any details about Vartanian's grades. However, in its opening appellate brief, the school explained:

> On or about October 20, 2014, plaintiff/appellant, Michael H. Vartanian (hereinafter, "Vartanian"), began the four-year law study program of defendant/appellee, Northwestern California University School of Law (hereinafter, "NWCU").
>
> The grade point average ("GPA") achieved by Vartanian for his second-year of studies at NWCU was 1.93. Because his GPA was below 2.0, Vartanian was placed on academic probation in accordance with school policy.
>
> Vartanian's third year of study began on December 30, 2016 and ended on December 29, 2017. His GPA for the third year was 1.55. In accordance with NWCU policy, students whose GPA falls below the minimum retention standards for two consecutive final grading periods must be academically dismissed. Because Vartanian failed to achieve a minimum 2.0 GPA for both the second and third years of study, he was academically dismissed following the calculation of his final course grades for the third year.
>
> Vartanian was dismissed from the law study program at NWCU for no other reason than his poor academic performance. On January 31, 2018, a letter of dismissal was transmitted to Vartanian by NWCU.

Appellee's Opposition Brief of Northwestern California University School of Law, Vartanian v. State B. of Cal., No. 18-16084, 2019 WL 2317612, at *5 (9th Cir. May 23, 2019).

304 *Vartanian*, 2018 WL 2724343 at *1.

305 *Id.* at *7

306 *Id.* at *1.

307 *Vartanian*, 794 F. App'x at 600-01.

308 Civil Case No. 18-00583 (RJL), 2019 WL 481643 (D.D.C. Feb. 7, 2019).

309 *Id.* at *2.

310 *Id.* at *5 (quoting Bain v. Howard Univ., 968 F. Supp. 2d 294, 300 (D.D.C. 2013)).

311 Civil Action No. 19-40062-DHH, 2021 WL 2785047 (D. Mass. Mar. 31, 2021).

312 *Id.* at *2 (indicating that Brown received the following grades: "B-," "C+," "C-," and "F").

313 *Id.*

314 *See id.* at *1.

315 *See id.* at *5-7 and *9.

316 *See id.* at *8-9.

Chapter 6

POST-1970 EXPULSION CASES—CHEATING

The second largest group of modern expulsion cases involves students expelled for cheating.[1]

In *In re Lamberis*,[2] for example, Anthony B. Lamberis, a practicing lawyer, was expelled from Northwestern University's LL.M. program after the school discovered he had plagiarized 47 pages of his 93-page thesis on privacy law.[3] Following his expulsion, the school filed a complaint with the Illinois Attorney Registration and Disciplinary Commission.[4]

"The Hearing Board recommended censure; the Review Board recommended suspension for six months; and the Administrator argue[d] for disbarment."[5] In deciding that censure was the appropriate punishment, the Illinois Supreme Court wrote:

> All honest scholars are the real victims in this case. The respondent's plagiarism showed disrespect for their legitimate pursuits. Moreover, the respondent's conduct undermined the honor system that is maintained in all institutions of learning. These harms, however, are rather diffuse, and in any event, Northwestern University has already rectified them by expelling the respondent, an act which will also undoubtedly ensure that the respondent will be hereafter excluded from the academic world.
>
> In view of the respondent's apparently unblemished record in the practice of law and the disciplinary sanctions which have already been imposed by Northwestern University, we choose censure as the most appropriate discipline for the respondent.[6]

Believing that a censure was insufficient punishment, Justice Underwood, joined by Justice Moran, dissented:

> Because of the calculated nature of respondent's misconduct some suspension seems to me necessary. Since the length of a suspension should bear a close relationship to the harm or risk of harm caused . . ., and since respondent's misconduct did not directly affect any other person, I would think a three-month suspension appropriate.[7]

In *McMillan v. Hunt*,[8] Jacqueline McMillan, a first-year student, was expelled from the University of Akron's law school after she was found to have plagiarized a research paper in her Basic Legal Communications class.[9] When McMillan sued for reinstatement, the district court dismissed her lawsuit.[10] In affirming its decision, the Sixth Circuit wrote:

> We find that McMillan received sufficient process to prevent an erroneous deprivation. The record indicates that McMillan received notice of the charges that were being brought against her in a hearing before the law school's Disciplinary Committee. At the two-day meeting, McMillan was represented by two attorneys and had ample opportunity to present her evidence in considerable detail. Each side had an opportunity to call witnesses and present their version of the events. . . .
>
> McMillan also argues that she was denied due process because of bias on the part of [Professor Richard] Grant, the Disciplinary Committee Chair, and Timothy Sheriden, a student representative on the Disciplinary Committee. . . . We find no evidence of actual bias in the record on the part of Grant or Sheriden.
>
> McMillan also argues that the law school violated her constitutional right to substantive due process by arbitrarily and capriciously dismissing her from law school. . . . From our review of the record, we can find no basis upon which to hold that the law school's actions were arbitrary or capricious. We find that the law school had

a rational basis for dismissing McMillan. The record supports the Disciplinary Committee's finding.[11]

In *Kellon v. Cleveland Marshall College of Law*,[12] Constance O. Kellon, a third-year student, "was suspended for a semester due to an academic citation. This suspension resulted in expulsion because of the expiration of the eight-year period permitted for completion of a law degree."[13] When Kellon sued for reinstatement, claiming that her age (64) made expulsion too harsh a penalty, the school successfully moved to have the case dismissed.[14] In partially reversing the trial court's decision, the Ohio Court of Appeals wrote:

> The appellant asserts one assignment of error:
> "The court of common pleas erred in holding that it did not have jurisdiction to decide plaintiff's claim for damages and allegations of violation of due process and equal protection under the Constitution of the state of Ohio and the Constitution of the United States of America."

> . . . .

> Since this court must accept all the allegations of the appellant's complaint as true, and further must bear in mind that the Civil Rules require only notice pleading, . . . and since the appellant's complaint raises federal constitutional claims, it must be concluded that the trial court erred in dismissing the federal claims set forth in the complaint.
> The appellant's assignment of error is well taken as to the federal constitutional claims, and overruled as to the state constitutional claims.[15]

In *Matter of Harper*,[16] Glyne L. Harper was expelled from Pace University's LL.M. program after the school discovered he had plagiarized a paper on energy law.[17] Harper subsequently failed to disclose on his bar application "that he had attended Pace University School of Law and that he had failed to receive a degree."[18] When his omission was discovered several years later, the New York Appellate Division censured Harper but declined to impose a more severe penalty because of his "expressed remorse, the isolated nature of his misconduct, and the uniformly high regard in which he is held by teachers, colleagues, and clients."[19]

In *Pfouts v. North Carolina Central University*,[20] Felicia S. Pfouts, a second-year law student, was expelled after she was found guilty of attempting to cheat on her Sales and Secured Transactions final exam.[21] When her numerous efforts to be readmitted proved fruitless,[22] she sued the school for negligence, unjust enrichment, and violations of her civil rights (under 42 U.S.C. § 1983) and educational rights (under 20 U.S.C. § 1232).[23] In response, the school successfully moved for dismissal based on sovereign immunity.[24] On appeal, the Fourth Circuit, in a one-paragraph opinion, affirmed: "We have reviewed the record and find no reversible error."[25]

In *Kerr v. Board of Regents of the University of Nebraska*,[26] upperclassman Michael M. Kerr was expelled after the law school's honor committee found him guilty of "four 'exceedingly flagrant' instances of plagiarism."[27] To gain readmission, Kerr, relying on Nebraska's Administrative Procedure Act ("NAPA"), filed suit against the school and asked the trial court to "reverse and vacate the decisions of the Honor Committee and Dean [Steven L.] Willborn."[28]

In granting the school's motion to dismiss, the trial court found "that it did not have jurisdiction under the [NAPA]."[29] In affirming this decision, the Nebraska Court of Appeals wrote:

> [T]here is no law requiring that the question of whether Kerr remains a College of Law student be determined by an agency . . . and, in any event . . . the Honor Committee and the dean are not agencies under [the NAPA]. Therefore, the district court correctly determined that it

did not have jurisdiction under the [NAPA], and as a result, neither do we.[30]

In *Al-Turk v. University of Nebraska*,[31] Layth M. Al-Turk was expelled after the law school's honor court found him guilty of committing plagiarism.[32] At the time of his expulsion, Al-Turk had completed 81 of the 111 credits he needed to graduate.[33] Believing he had been treated more harshly than similarly situated White students (due to the fact that he was both an Arab and a Muslim),[34] Al-Turk sued the school for violating his federal and state constitutional rights.[35]

Along with his complaint, Al-Turk filed a motion for a TRO.[36] In finding that Al-Turk was not entitled to a TRO, the court wrote:

> [A]t this early stage of the proceedings, it is not "probable"
> that Plaintiff will prevail on the merits. . . . It is hard to believe that
> Defendants' discriminated against Plaintiff because of his protected
> status. The uncontradicted evidence shows that, after failing to
> maintain his grades, Plaintiff was readmitted to the law school on
> probation about two months before this dispute first arose. In other
> words, the leniency with which Plaintiff was treated in August of
> 2012 strongly rebuts any suggestion that the final dismissal decision
> in February of 2013 was driven by religious, racial or ethnic animus.
> Moreover, even if the Honor Code is construed to have prohibited the
> prosecutor from using the recorded recollection of the complaining
> professor about a conversation with Plaintiff held after the charge was
> made but before Plaintiff knew of the charge, in every other respect
> Plaintiff was provided with all the process he was due. Just as no trial
> is perfect, no Honor Code prosecution is likely to be perfect. Simply
> put, the Due Process Clause does not require perfection.[37]

In *Beauchene v. Mississippi College*,[38] Mark Beauchene was expelled after committing two acts of plagiarism in less than a year.[39] Following his expulsion, Beauchene sued for breach of contract and intentional and negligent infliction of emotional distress.[40] In finding Beauchene's lawsuit to be baseless, the district court wrote:

> On this record, there can be only one conclusion: Beauchene
> engaged in widespread plagiarism in violation of MC Law's Honor
> Code, and the procedures extended and provided to him during
> the investigation of those charges were fundamentally fair. Neither
> the decision to suspend him nor to expel him was arbitrary and
> capricious.
>
> In all respects, the Court finds that MC Law acted appropriately.[41]

In *Carney v. University of Akron*,[42] Caitlin Carney, a third-year student at the University of Akron, was accused of plagiarizing a paper she had submitted to satisfy both her J.D. writing requirement and her LL.M. thesis requirement. At a hearing before the law school's Student Discipline Committee ("SDC"), Carney admitted she was guilty and apologized. Despite her contrition, the SDC, by a 4-3 vote, recommended that she be expelled. This recommendation was adopted by Dean Matthew J. Wilson.[43]

Believing she had been treated unfairly, Carney filed a federal lawsuit in which she accused the law school, Wilson, and Professor Carolyn L. Dessin, the SDC's chair, of violating the Due Process Clause, 42 U.S.C. § 1983, the ADA, Section 504 of the Rehabilitation Act of 1973, and Ohio statutory and common law. Finding none of these claims to be colorable, the district court granted summary judgment in favor of the defendants.[44]

In addition to holding that Wilson and Dessin enjoyed qualified immunity[45] and that Carney had never asked for an accommodation under the ADA,[46] the court emphasized that the law school's process had been constitutionally sufficient:

> [T]he [First Amended Complaint] is devoid of any factual allegations
> that, if believed, would suggest defendant Dessin, or any other member

of the Committee, had a bias such that the presumption of honesty and integrity in the proceedings would be overcome. . . .

As to [Carney's] conclusory allegation that her appeal was "summarily" denied without reference to her specific arguments, it is both irrelevant and inaccurate. . . . In a multi-page decision, Wilson specifically addressed plaintiff's arguments—including "'mitigating factors' including overextending [herself] during [her] third year of law school while experiencing significant health challenges." . . . While defendant Wilson "empathize[d] with [her] physical struggles" he found that her dishonest and unethical conduct was "unacceptable[,]" and warranted expulsion. . . . Plaintiff was afforded a full and fair opportunity to present an alternative version of the facts, which included her position on mitigation, and the Due Process Clause requires no more.[47]

In *Chen v. Lowe*,[48] Christopher M. Grande and Eric Lowe were expelled from the University of Louisville's law school after it was discovered that Lowe had written a term paper for Grande.[49] When his subsequent request for readmission was denied,[50] Lowe sued the school and Dean James M. Chen in their official and individual capacities for breach of contract, fraud, misrepresentation, and unjust enrichment.[51]

The trial court granted summary judgment to the school and Chen in their official capacities,[52] but denied Chen's motion to dismiss in his individual capacity after finding that genuine issues of material fact existed "as to whether Chen acted outside the scope of his authority as Dean by conducting his own investigation of [Lowe's] conduct, by circumventing the procedures set forth in the student handbook, and by rejecting the proposed settlement agreement he had helped induce. . . ."[53]

In dismissing Chen's appeal, the Kentucky Court of Appeals wrote:

The circuit court's order found that it could not resolve the issue of Dean Chen's qualification for immunity based on the issues presented in the pleadings, even when construed in a light most favorable to Eric. Having reviewed the record, we agree with this determination. At the current juncture, the factual issues remain unresolved and the immunity question remains open. We will not overstep our bounds by attempting to make findings of fact on those issues so we can determine an immunity question that the circuit court has not yet fully addressed.[54]

Lastly, in *Tinsman v. Carry*,[55] Claudine C. Tinsman, a first-year student, was expelled from the University of Southern California's law school after it discovered she had cheated off another student (Irina A. Kirnosova) during its spring law journal write-on competition.[56] When Tinsman sued, the trial court ordered the school to conduct further hearings.[57] After it did so, it again decided that Tinsman should be expelled.[58]

Believing that the school had failed to properly consider her claim of mental illness, Tinsman filed an objection to the school's request that Tinsman's case be closed.[59] In siding with the school, the trial court found that the school had "reconsidered its decision consistent with the court's order."[60] In affirming this decision, the California Court of Appeals wrote:

> [USC's Student Behavior Appeals Panel] explained that its policy was to impose sanctions on students that corresponded to the severity of their actions, and that would hold students accountable for their actions. "Here," the Panel found, "Ms. Tinsman's actions included: lying to a fellow student to obtain access to her computer, accessing the student's work, copying that work and misrepresenting it as her own, hacking into the student's email account, submitting a false admission on behalf of that student, repeatedly lying to University authorities during the course of the investigation, and causing harm to a fellow student." The Panel concluded no sanction lesser than expulsion could adequately redress these actions that included

criminal acts. The Panel thus concluded that "[f]or all the above-stated reasons, even though Ms. Tinsman's mental illness evidence was new and credible, the [Panel] has reconsidered the evidence pursuant to the court's order and statement of decision, and concludes that expulsion is the appropriate sanction."

. . . .

The Panel adequately set forth its reasoning on all of Tinsman's evidence purporting to demonstrate a causal link between her mental disorder and her misconduct. Its determination that expulsion remained the only sufficient sanction, given the severity of Tinsman's dishonesty and misconduct, was reasonable. We conclude the trial court did not err in concluding that USC had complied with the writ.[61]

1   As will be seen, many of the cases in this chapter involve plagiarism. For a general discussion of plagiarism, see Judge Richard A. Posner's *The Little Book of Plagiarism* (2007). Curiously, Judge Posner does not discuss plagiarism by law students.

2   443 N.E.2d 549 (Ill. 1982).

3   *Id.* at 550.

4   *Id.*

5   *Id.* at 552.

6   *Id.* at 552-53.

7   *Id.* at 553.

8   968 F.2d 1215 (table), No. 91-3843, 1992 WL 168827 (6th Cir. July 21, 1992), *cert. denied,* 506 U.S. 1050 (1993).

9   *Id.* at *1.

10 *Id.*

11 *Id.* at *1-2.

12 657 N.E.2d 835 (Ohio Ct. App. 1995).

13 *Id.* at 836. According to the court, Kellon "was suspended and given a non[-]passing grade by the Honor Council of the school[.]" *Id.* The court does not specify why Kellon was punished.

14 *Id.*

15 *Id.* at 836-38. There is no further public reporting about the case. In her obituary, there is no mention of Kellon becoming a lawyer. *See Constance O. Kellon,* Clev. Plain Dealer, Dec. 7, 2011, *at* https:// obits.cleveland.com/us/obituaries/cleveland/name/constance-kellon-obituary?id=24450189.

16 645 N.Y.S.2d 846 (App. Div. 1996).

17 *Id.* at 847 (explaining that Harper eventually entered into an agreement with the school admitting his guilt and stipulating that he was barred from re-entering the LL.M. program).

18 *Id.*

19 *Id.* at 847-48.

20 No. 1:02CV00016, 2003 WL 1562412 (M.D.N.C. Mar. 24, 2003), *aff'd,* 68 F. App'x 505 (4th Cir. 2003).

21 *Id.* at *1-2.

22 *Id.* at *2 (explaining that Pfouts's had pursued "a multi-tiered appeals process" that ended only after her entreaties were rejected by the University of North Carolina's Board of Governors).

23 *Id.* at *3.

24 *Id.* at *5 ("To avoid the Eleventh Amendment, Plaintiff must invoke a federal statute that abrogates North Carolina's sovereign immunity. Plaintiff principally relies on § 1983 to accomplish this task. As the Supreme Court held in *Quern v. Jordan,* [440 U.S. 332 (1979),] however, § 1983 does not abrogate Eleventh Amendment immunity") (footnotes omitted).

25 *Pfouts,* 68 F. App'x at 506.

26 739 N.W.2d 224 (Neb. Ct. App. 2007).

27 *Id.* at 226. According to the court, Kerr submitted three plagiarized papers in three different courses—Independent Research, International Human Rights Law, and Law and Medicine—and plagiarized from himself in his Law and Medicine course by using parts of his International Human Rights Law paper without obtaining the permission of either professor. *Id.*

28 *Id.* at 227.

29 *Id.*

30 *Id.* at 229.

31 No. 8:13CV74, 2013 WL 959223 (D. Neb. Mar. 12, 2013), *later proceedings at* No. 8:13CV74, 2013 WL 1399040 (D. Neb. Apr. 5, 2013).

32 *Al-Turk*, 2013 WL 959223, at *1 ("Evidence from Defendants showed that Plaintiff had been readmitted to law school on probation in August of 2012 after previously failing to keep up his grades. In the fall of 2012, other evidence showed that Plaintiff copied almost verbatim and without attribution materials from two texts and submitted that information as part of his class work. There is a strong showing that Plaintiff was guilty of plagiarism. The evidence also tends to show that Plaintiff may have lied to his professor about the paper that contained the plagiarized material, although that evidence is less strong.").

33 *Id.*

34 *Id.* at *2.

35 *Id.* at *1.

36 *Id.*

37 *Id.* at *3. Subsequently, the magistrate judge assigned to the case refused to recuse herself and granted the school's request to move the trial from Omaha to Lincoln. *See Al-Turk*, 2013 WL 1399040, at *3. A short time later, the case settled. *See* Kevin Abourezk, *NU, Law Student Settle Lawsuit*, Lincoln J. Star (Neb.), May 1, 2013, at B3 (reporting that the settlement required the school "to release its claim against [Al-Turk] for $3,018 in tuition for the spring 2013 semester [but allows] the university . . . to inform other academic institutions and state bar associations that Al-Turk was dismissed because of honor code violations."). Rather than try to finish his degree elsewhere, Al-Turk went into business and now works as a medical recruiter in Omaha. *See Layth Al-Turk*, LinkedIn, *at* https://www.linkedin.com/in/layth-al-turk-ba99b024/ (last visited Apr. 1, 2022).

38 986 F. Supp. 2d 755 (S.D. Miss. 2013).

39 *Id.* at 758. Both acts came as part of Beauchene's attempt to complete an independent study project, first for Professor Cynthia L.

Nicoletti and then for Professor Cecile C. Edwards. Beauchene committed his first act of plagiarism in the Spring of 2012, when he was a second-year student. *Id.* at 759. After being allowed to continue his studies, he committed his second act of plagiarism in the Fall of 2012. *Id.* at 762. In his memo advising Beauchene that he was being expelled, Dean Matthew Steffey wrote:

> [I]n submitting your writing requirement paper this semester, you once again committed significant and serious acts of plagiarism. As before, you used a computer to 'copy and paste' text from various Internet sources. And, as before, you used this work of other authors without proper attribution to the true source of the text. Indeed, long passages of your paper are taken word-for-word from uncited internet sources without any attribution whatever. . . .
>
> Given your prior suspension for this same conduct, and the clear and unambiguous instructions and warnings from the course professor orally and in writing, this lack of candor only confirms a culpable state of mind. Indeed, given the extent of the plagiarism, and the nature of some of the plagiarized sources, the only credible conclusion is that your misconduct was fully willful, and taken with full knowledge that it constituted academic dishonesty of the 'most blatant' form as described by the Honor Code.

Id. at 762-63.

40 *Id.* at 759.

41 *Id.* at 775-76.

42 Case No. 5:15-cv-2309, 2016 WL 4036726 (N.D. Ohio July 28, 2016), *appeal dismissed for lack of prosecution*, Case No. 16-3993, 2016 WL 9610018 (6th Cir. Dec. 1, 2016). To protect her reputation, Carney initially sought to sue as a "Jane Doe" but her request to do so was denied. *See* Doe v. University of Akron, Case No. 5:15-cv-2309, 2016 WL 4520512 (N.D. Ohio, Feb. 3, 2016).

43 *Carney*, 2016 WL 4036726 at *4.

44 *Id.* at *1.

45 *Id.* at *12-14.

46 *Id.* at *14-16.

47 *Id.* at *10-11. Even though she did not receive them, Carney, who now works as a law clerk in Youngstown, Ohio, continues to list her "J.D./LL.M." on her *LinkedIn* page. *See Caitlin Carney,* LinkedIn, *at* https://www.linkedin.com/in/caitycarney/ (last visited Apr. 1, 2022).

48 521 S.W.3d 587 (Ky. Ct. App. 2017).

49 *Id.* at 588-89.

At the time of the duo's deception, Grande, 49, was a highly accomplished anesthesiologist who had published numerous books and articles and had testified before Congress. In 2017, while still battling the school, Grande died at his vacation home in Colorado. *See* University of Louisville v. Grande, Nos. 2014-CA-001268-MR, 2014-CA-001527-MR, and 2015-CA-000512-MR, 2018 WL 1995958, at *1 (Ky. Ct. App. Apr. 27, 2018); *Obituaries—Grande, Christopher,* Herald-Leader (Lexington, KY), Jan. 5, 2017, at 5A; *Christopher Rocco Michael Grande,* Find-A-Grave, *at* https://www.findagrave. com/memorial/187580075/christopher-rocco_michael-grande (last visited Apr. 1, 2022). *See also Testimony of Christopher M. Grande Before the U.S. Senate—Committee on Environment and Public Works—Subcommittee on Clean Air, Wetlands, Private Property and Nuclear Safety* (Apr. 29, 1997), *available at* https://www.epw.senate. gov/105th/gra_4-29.htm (giving Grande's background).

50 Lowe was accused in September 2010 and expelled in March 2011. At the time of his expulsion, Lowe was told that he could apply for re-admission after three years. In March 2014, Lowe's petition for re-admission was denied by the university's board of trustees "without explanation." *Chen,* 521 S.W.3d at 589.

51 *Id.* at 589-90.

52 *See* Lowe v. Univ. of Louisville, Civil Action No. 14-CI-476 (Franklin Cir. Ct. June 15, 2015), *at* http://juryverdicts.net/ChenvLouisville. pdf. This decision is not officially reported and is not available on either Lexis or Westlaw.

53 *Chen*, 521 S.W.3d at 590.

54 *Id.* at 591. It is not known what became of Lowe's lawsuit. In any event, Lowe did not return to the law school and never became a lawyer. *See Eric Lowe*, LINKEDIN, *at* https://www.linkedin.com/in/ ericloweaptiva/ (last visited Apr. 1, 2022) (indicating that Lowe currently is the chief executive officer of "an independent multi-specialty medical group with locations throughout Kentucky").

55 B283418, 2019 WL 1325087 (Cal. Ct. App. Mar. 25, 2019).

56 *Id.* at *1, *6. Kirnosova ended up receiving an offer from the school's *Interdisciplinary Law Journal* and later served as its managing editor. *See Irina Kirnosova*, MATERN LAW GROUP, *at* https://www.maternlawgroup.com/our-firm/our-people/irina-kirnosova/ (last visited Apr. 1, 2022).

Tinsman might have gotten away with her deception had she not included in her paper an unusual parenthetical that Kirnosova had used in her submission:

> Each student's parenthetical stated: "The Bluebook: A Uniform System of Citation R. 18.2, at 165-70 (Columbia Law Review Ass'n et al. eds., 19th ed. 2010) (making it hell on Earth to figure out how to cite to an annual report that is only available online, to resist throwing The Bluebook at the nearest passer-by, and to keep from calling up Columbia Law Review Association to demand 'Dunkin' Donuts' for my pain and suffering)."

. . . .

One of Tinsman's explanations for her purported reference to Dunkin' Donuts in the parenthetical was that she had been eating Dunkin' Donuts while she worked on her write-on assignment.

"When [Donna Budar-Turner, the school's investigator] asked how she was able to acquire Dunkin' Donuts during the very busy Write-On competition, given the fact that there were no Dunkin' Donut franchises anywhere in Los Angeles County during the time period in question, Ms. Tinsman reported that a friend 'brings' Dunkin' Donuts to her. When asked to elaborate on her response, Ms. Tinsman reported that 'an old friend from undergrad' gave them to her. When asked for the name of that friend, Ms. Tinsman replied, 'Richard Chavales.' Ms. Tinsman later reported that Mr. Chavales mailed the donuts to her. . . . Although Ms. Tinsman had her cell phone and computer in her possession during her meeting with [Ms. Budar-Turner], when asked to provide contact informa-tion for Mr. Chavales so [that Ms. Budar-Turner] could verify Ms. Tinsman's report, Ms. Tinsman declined to do so. . . . An internet search on October 17, 2014 for 'Richard Chavales' returned 'no results.'"

"Nearly two weeks later, on October 30, 2014, [Ms. Budar-Turner] received email correspondence from rchavales@gmail.com. The correspondence purports to be from 'Richard Chavales' and attempts to corroborate Ms. Tinsman's report. . . . The email claims that Mr. Chavales purchased Dunkin' Donuts from outside of Los Angeles County a day before he was scheduled to travel to Los Angeles to visit Ms. Tinsman. The email explains that the evening before he was to leave for Los Angeles, Mr. Chavales suddenly had to cancel his visit. The message states that after calling Ms. Tinsman after 5:00 p.m. to cancel the visit, Mr. Chavales decided to mail the donuts to her 'since [he] had already bought the donuts.' [Ms. Budar-Turner] has not been able to determine the truth, verac-ity or authenticity of the correspondence or the true identity of the author despite repeated requests for contact information and a copy of a government issued photo ID from the sender. The email was therefore not deemed credible or reliable."

Tinsman, 2019 WL 1325087, at *3.

57 *Id.* at *7.

58 *Id.* at *9.

59 *Id.*

60 *Id.*

61 *Id.* at *14. For a further look at the case, see Staci Zaretsky, *Law Student Expelled After Trying to Lie, Cheat, and Hack Her Way onto Law Review*, ABOVE THE LAW, Mar. 28, 2019, *at* https://abovethelaw.com/2019/03/law-student-expelled-after-trying-to-lie-cheat-and-hack-her-way-onto-law-review/.

Chapter 7

POST-1970 EXPULSION CASES—INAPPROPRIATE, DANGEROUS, OR CRIMINAL BEHAVIOR

Law schools sometimes are forced to expel students for inappropriate, dangerous, or criminal behavior ("IDCB").[1] In earlier eras, IDCB tended to involve cursing, drugs, fighting, or political protests.[2] In more modern times, IDCB has expanded to include computer misuse, hate crimes, and sexual misconduct.[3]

Like other types of expulsions, IDCB expulsions sometimes lead to lawsuits. In *Keys v. Sawyer*,[4] for example, J.B. Keys was expelled from Texas Southern University's law school for "publishing and distributing false and libelous statements concerning" two faculty members.[5] In response, Keys sued the school, which moved for, and received, summary judgment.[6] After exhausting his appeals, Keys brought a new federal lawsuit asserting the same claims.[7] Once again, the district court granted the school's motion for summary judgment:

> [P]laintiff's actions must fail for the obvious reason that these identical issues have been previously litigated by these same parties. Under the doctrine of "res judicata," a judgment on the merits in a prior suit involving the same parties or their privies bars a second suit based on the same cause of action.[8]

In *Cloud v. Trustees of Boston University*,[9] Leevonn Cloud, a third-year student, "was charged with . . . peeping under the skirts of women students in the university library . . . while crawling on all fours under [the] tables where the women were seated."[10] After the school expelled him, Cloud sued it for breach of contract and breach of privacy.[11] In response, the school moved for, and was granted, summary judgment.[12] On appeal, the First Circuit affirmed:

> Since we find Cloud's challenges to his disciplinary hearing insubstantial, we uphold the grant of summary judgment on his breach of contract claim. . . .
>
> We now consider Cloud's claim that the university violated his statutory right to privacy by placing the transcript of his prior rape trial on file for the student body to review. . . . Cloud himself revealed his conviction on January 18, 1982 in publicly resigning from the presidency of the Student Bar Association. The law school dean made the transcript public on February 3, 1982. Further, the transcript was a public record available from the Maryland courts. Given these facts, the university did not violate Cloud's privacy rights by placing the transcript in an open file. Thus the district court did not err in granting summary judgment on Cloud's privacy claim.[13]

In *Warren v. Drake University*,[14] Mark L. Warren was suspended after he was arrested for attempting to use a stolen credit card at a store in Des Moines.[15] After pleading guilty, serving one year's probation, and having his record expunged,[16] he sought to be readmitted so that he could finish his last year of law school.[17] When the school refused to take him back,[18] Warren filed a lawsuit

> alleging violations of his constitutional rights, breach of contract, and that the law school's actions were arbitrary, capricious, and in bad faith. The district court dismissed plaintiff's constitutional claims and his claims against individual school officials, but denied summary judgment on plaintiff's contract and bad faith claims against the University, which were tried to a jury at plaintiff's request.[19]

The jury sided with the school on both counts.[20] Abandoning his bad faith claim, Warren appealed just his contract claim to the Eighth Circuit.[21] It found no reversible error:

> If construing the contract as a matter of law, we might well have reached a different result than the jury in this case, but because plaintiff elected to have a jury construe his contract with the University in determining whether the University's actions constituted a breach of that contract, and because the record on appeal precludes our review of the sufficiency of the evidence in support of the jury's verdict that no breach of contract occurred, the judgment of the district court against plaintiff is in all respects affirmed.[22]

In *Czarsty v. University of Bridgeport School of Law*,[23] Keith J. Czarsty was arrested during his second semester for counterfeiting.[24] Following his conviction in federal court, the law school expelled him.[25] Czarsty subsequently filed a four-count complaint against the school and demanded a jury trial.[26] When the school moved to strike Czarsty's case from the jury docket, the Connecticut Superior Court rejected its request:

> In framing count one (deprivation of property right) and count two (breach of contract to educate), Czarsty alleged that he has no adequate remedy at law. Thus, those two counts sound only in equity. His fourth count is framed in unjust enrichment, which is essentially an equitable action. . . .
>
> The architecture of the CUTPA [Connecticut Unfair Trade Practices Act] claim in count three is another matter. Here, Czarsty has alleged that the Law School by its proceedings leading to its expulsion order deprived him of a "property right" and breached its contract to educate him. Deprivation of property rights was cognizable for a jury in this state prior to 1818 as was a claim for breach of contract. . . .

We conclude that the issues presented by Czarsty in count three pursuant to the Connecticut Unfair Trade Practices Act involve rights and remedies (damages) rooted in our common law and are justiciable before a jury prior to 1818 in this state. Consequently, we deny the motion to strike from the jury docket.[27]

In *Jarzynka v. St. Thomas University School of Law*,[28] Richard Jarzynka, a first-year student, was expelled after he threatened "to blow-up the Legal Writing Department" and publicly announced he had compiled a "hit list" that included his Torts professor Ediberto Román.[29] Jarzynka subsequently filed an 11-count complaint against the school.[30] After the resolution of various preliminary matters,[31] the case boiled down to a single question: "[Did] the University arbitrarily expel[] the Plaintiff[?]"[32] In deciding the answer was "no," the district court wrote:

> Having carefully reviewed the record, the Court finds that the Plaintiff has failed to meet his burden on summary judgment to bring forward facts that create a genuine dispute as to whether the University arbitrarily exercised its power. . . . Defendant has brought forward undisputed evidence that two students, [Michele] Vargas and [Anthony] Tinelli, came to the administration with safety concerns of a serious and imminent nature. Defendant has brought forward evidence that at the same time student [Rosalind] Griffie informed the University that Plaintiff had a prior history of being "Baker Acted" twice and had been self-medicating. . . . The University has also brought forward undisputed evidence that Plaintiff acted in a threatening manner towards Professor Roman, as alleged by the students who approached the University. Furthermore, it is undisputed that Defendant offered Plaintiff a post-expulsion hearing on five (5) separate occasions, which included an opportunity to present witnesses, state his case, and be represented by counsel. The undisputed facts indicate that the University had cause to immediately expel the Plaintiff given reasonable concerns of an imminent safety threat to the

Law School community, and that the University offered Plaintiff basic procedural protections to challenge his expulsion via a post-expulsion administrative hearing. The Court therefore finds that the Plaintiff has not created a genuine dispute as to whether the University's decision was arbitrary.[33]

On appeal, the Eleventh Circuit affirmed in a one-sentence opinion: "After review and oral argument in this diversity action, the Court concludes that the district court properly granted summary judgment to the defendant St. Thomas University on the claims of the plaintiff Richard Jarzynka."[34]

In *Taranto v. Whittier College*,[35] Bradley S. Taranto, a first-year law student, was expelled for "bizarre, disruptive, and threatening behavior."[36] Subsequently, he filed a state lawsuit accusing the school of breach of contract, disability discrimination, intentional infliction of emotional distress, and slander.[37] He also sued an employment agency (Stride & Associates, Inc.) and a potential employer (stockbroker William O'Neil & Company, Inc.), claiming they had conspired against him after learning about his academic problems.[38]

The trial court initially dismissed Taranto's entire complaint, but the California Court of Appeal reinstated the claims against O'Neil and the school.[39] In response, Whittier *College* filed a motion for summary judgment, which the trial court granted and the Court of Appeal affirmed.[40] Taranto then sought to add Whittier *Law School*[41] as a new defendant, but the trial court granted Whittier's demurrer.[42]

In the meantime, a bench trial was held on Taranto's claim against O'Neil.[43] When the trial resulted in a judgment for O'Neil, Taranto appealed both it and the trial court's granting of Whittier's demurrer.[44] In finding the two decisions to be correct, the Court of Appeal wrote:

> The record reveals Taranto raised the identical issues in his lawsuit
> against "Whittier College," and these issues were litigated fully when
> the trial court granted Whittier's summary judgment on the merits.

Taranto made no showing that his proposed action against Whittier Law School was anything other than a duplication of his claims against Whittier College. . . .

[As for O'Neil] . . . Taranto has not directed us to any error or abuse of discretion.[45]

In *Doe v. Loyola University*,[46] "John Doe," a part-time student at Loyola-New Orleans law school,[47] was expelled for dating violence.[48] When he sued the school for violating his federal civil rights, as well as for various contract and tort claims under state law, the school moved for summary judgment.[49] In granting the school's motion, the court wrote in pertinent part:

[Doe] admitted that dating violence, of which he was twice found "responsible," would not be condoned by Loyola, violated [its] conduct policy, and would lead to disciplinary sanctions. Doe does not debate that he had an opportunity to be heard after an investigation and during a hearing. And he fails to identify any Code provision that Loyola disregarded in administering student discipline. Doe simply disagrees with the outcome of his disciplinary proceeding.[50]

Lastly, in *Syed v. Northwestern University*,[51] Fahad Syed, "a 31-year-old Muslim man with . . . bipolar disorder, ADHD, anxiety, and depression,"[52] was expelled from the law school after he attacked and threatened other students and stalked several staff members.[53] In rejecting Syed's requests for a preliminary injunction and a TRO,[54] the district court wrote:

The relevant question, however, is not whether Northwestern's disciplinary process reached the right conclusion or consulted all the appropriate evidence. It is whether the process was corrupted by a discriminatory motive. Putting Syed's conclusory statements to the side, the record does not suggest that Northwestern's given reasons for expelling him were pretextual. . . .

Alternatively, Syed seems to suggest that he cannot be held accountable for acts that were caused by his disability. Federal law, however, does not prohibit individuals from being punished for misconduct arising from their disability, so long as the individual is not being punished for the disability itself. . . . Northwestern expelling Syed because it believes he assaulted and harassed other students . . . does not violate the ADA or Section 504.[55]

1   In 1983, for example, the University of Hawaii ("UH") expelled Ross
    M. Segawa, a third-year law student, for orchestrating a scheme to
    illegally register voters to help him get elected to the Hawaii House
    of Representatives. Nine other UH law students were given lesser
    punishments for helping Segawa. *See* June Watanabe, *Segawa is Ex-
    pelled from UH*, Honolulu Star-Bull., May 6, 1983, at A1. Sega-
    wa subsequently was sentenced to a year in prison and 325 hours
    of community service. *See* Gerald Kato & Ken Kobayashi, *Segawa,
    Wife Sentenced in Voter Fraud*, Honolulu Advert., Aug. 18, 1984, at
    A1. In 2001, Governor Benjamin J. Cayetano pardoned Segawa. *See*
    Richard Borreca, *Gov's Pardon Eases Pain of Vote Scandal*, Honolulu
    Star-Bull., Sept. 5, 2001, at A2. *See also Ross Segawa*, LinkedIn,
    at https://www.linkedin.com/in/ross-segawa-96a71432/ (indicating
    that Segawa currently works as a Honolulu real estate agent).

2   In 1857, for example, the University of Mississippi's law school ex-
    pelled James G. Minter after he "fought an undergraduate student,
    Robert F. Wilson, over the attention of a woman." *See* Alexander M.
    Heideman, *Dangerous Subjects in Every Sense: Violence and Politics at
    the Law Department of the University of Mississippi*, 89 Miss. L.J. 407,
    425-26 (2020) (noting that Minter was let back in after his classmates
    protested his expulsion).

    In 1937, John C. Harrison was expelled from the University of
    Montana's law school for cursing at one of his professors while de-
    manding a grade change. *See Charles S. Johnson, John C. Harrison:
    Former Justice Dies at 98*, Missoulinan (Missoula, MT), Nov. 12,
    2011, at B3 (reporting that after he was expelled, Harrison earned

his law degree at George Washington University and ended up spending 34 years on the Montana Supreme Court).

In 1960, Southern University's law school expelled John W. Johnson, Kenneth L. Johnson, and Donald T. Moss after they participated "in a sit-in at a [Baton Rouge] whites-only lunch counter." *See* Steve Seidenberg, *Historic Sit-In—44 Years Later*, 3 No. 20 ABA J. E-Rep., May 21, 2004, at 2 ("At the time, the school's disciplinary committee characterized their behavior as 'conduct unbecoming a student.' Now, the university calls their actions 'heroic efforts for civil rights,' and is creating a one-hour documentary to be broadcast on PBS on the sit-in and its aftermath.").

In 1963, the University of Mississippi's law school expelled Cleve McDowell, its first Black student, after he was found guilty of carrying a concealed weapon. McDowell explained, to no avail, that he did not feel safe walking to class. *See Student Fined $100 on Pistol Charge*, Richmond Times-Dispatch (VA), Sept. 29, 1963, at 18A. *See also* McDowell v. State, 168 So. 2d 658 (Miss. 1964) (dismissing McDowell's appeal of his conviction). Although McDowell was not readmitted, he was able to finish his studies at Texas Southern University's law school and later became an esteemed civil rights lawyer in Mississippi. *See* Robert H. Smith, *Cleve McDowell Murder Stuns County, Friends*, Enter.-Tocsin (Indianola, MS), Mar. 20, 1997, at 1A, 12A (reporting on the killing of McDowell by one of his clients during a botched burglary of McDowell's home). (In recounting McDowell's expulsion from the University of Mississippi, this article states that McDowell had the pistol "in his coat pocket for protection. The gun fell out onto the law school porch steps.")

In 1970, David S. Milch, the creator of such television hits as *Deadwood* (HBO) and *NYPD Blue* (ABC), was expelled from Yale University's law school after a particularly bad LSD trip. *See* Harvey Blume, *Q & A with David Milch*, Boston Sun. Globe, Apr. 30, 2006, at E3 (explaining that "Milch had applied [to the law school] only in order to beat the Vietnam draft, but when his draft board learned his ejection involved drugs, a shotgun, blasted streetlights, and carloads of outraged New Haven police, it ruled that law school or not, this guy wasn't Army material.").

3   In 2011, for example, Brandon J. Winston, a Harvard University law student, was expelled after a classmate (Kamilah Willingham) accused him of sexual assault. After a four-year legal battle, Winston was found guilty of simple (*i.e.*, non-sexual) battery and assault and given probation. *See Brandon Winston on Trial,* BRANDON PROJECT, *at* https://brandonproject.org/ (last visited Apr. 1, 2022) (under "Legal Docs—Court Documents—Sentencing Hearing"). Subsequently, Winston was allowed to re-enroll at Harvard. When his story was included in the 2015 documentary *The Hunting Ground,* 19 faculty members issued a press release accusing the filmmakers of distorting the case's facts. *See* Michael Shammas, *19 Harvard Law Professors Defend Law Student Brandon Winston, Denouncing His Portrayal in "The Hunting Ground,"* HARV. L. REC., Nov. 13, 2015, *at* http://hlrecord.org/19-harvard-law-professors-defend-law-student-brandon-winston-denouncing-his-portrayal-in-the-hunting-ground/.   After graduating from Harvard in 2016, Winston was admitted to the California bar and now works as a freelance writer. *See Brandon Winston,* LINKEDIN, *at* https://www.linkedin.com/in/brandonjwinston/ (last visited Apr. 1, 2022). Willingham, on the other hand, has become a social justice advocate and in 2016 spearheaded the viral social media campaign #JustSaySorry. *See Kamilah Willingham: Writer—Speaker—Activist, at* http://www.kamilahwillingham.com/ (last visited Apr. 1, 2022).

In 2019, Oklahoma City University's law school expelled an already-suspended student after he posted White supremacist flyers around the campus (citing federal privacy laws, the school has declined to reveal the student's name). *See* Snejana Farberov, *Oklahoma Law School Student is Questioned by FBI Joint Terrorism Task Force and Expelled for Posting 'It's Okay to Be White' Flyers on Campus,* DAILY MAIL (London), Dec. 12, 2019, updated Nov. 1, 2020, *at* https://www.dailymail.co.uk/news/article-7786475/Oklahoma-law-school-student-expelled-posting-Okay-White-flyers-campus.html.

In a case that appeared after this book's closing date, a California Western School of Law student was expelled for:

> 1. Obtaining unauthorized access to the accounts of two other [law] students, on September 30th[,] 2017 and January 13th, 2018, and using those accounts to send inappropriate emails to a number of faculty and students as well as one alumnus. These were violations of the [the law school's student conduct code] both because of the misrepresentation of the identity of the sender and also because the emails were offensive or abusive in nature.

> 2. On both occasions using those accounts to print a number of items that were then charged to those students. These were violations of the [code] because they were tantamount to thefts from those other students.

Teacher v. California W. Sch. of L., 292 Cal. Rptr. 3d 343, 348-49 (Ct. App. 2022). Although the trial court entered judgment for the school, the California Court of Appeal reversed and remanded because the plaintiff had been denied the opportunity to cross-examine witnesses during his expulsion hearing. *Id.* at 362.

4   353 F. Supp. 936 (S.D. Tex. 1973), *aff'd mem.*, 496 F.2d 876 (5th Cir.), *cert. denied*, 419 U.S. 901 (1974).

5   *Id.* at 938. The court does not identify the professors and does not explain what caused Keys to have an issue with them.

6   *Id.*

7   *Id.*

8   *Id.* at 940.

9   720 F.2d 721 (1st Cir. 1983).

10   *Id.* at 723.

11   *Id.* at 724.

12 *Id.*

13 *Id.* at 726. For a further look at Cloud's 1972 rape conviction, see Cloud v. State, 287 A.2d 316 (Md. Ct. Spec. App.), *cert. denied,* 265 Md. 736 (1972).

Since his expulsion from law school, Cloud has worked as both a political organizer and as a taxicab driver. Both pursuits have landed him in court. *See* Cloud v. Community Works, 141 F.3d 1149 (table), No. 97-1796, 1998 WL 85282 (1st Cir. Feb. 25, 1998) (partially reinstating Cloud's racial discrimination suit against his former employer), *later proceedings at* 540 U.S. 852 (2003); Cloud v. Community Works, 762 N.E.2d 919 (table), No. 00-P-433, 2002 WL 230669 (Mass. App. Ct. Feb. 15, 2002), *review denied,* 768 N.E.2d 1086 (Mass. 2002) (upholding the dismissal of Cloud's racial discrimination suit against his former employer); Cloud v. Massachusetts Bay Transp. Auth., 891 N.E.2d 716 (table), No. 07-P-911, 2008 WL 2929024 (Mass. App. Ct. July 31, 2008) (rejecting Cloud's claim that a police officer violated his civil rights when he ordered Cloud's taxicab towed after discovering its registration had been revoked for lack of insurance). In 2013, Cloud self-published a book about his legal battles. *See* LEEVONN CLOUD, PRO SE: POCKET CHANGE VS. THE BENJAMINS (2013), *available at* https://www.amazon.com/Pro-Se-Pocket-Change-Benjamins-ebook/dp/B009SRII28.

14 886 F.2d 200 (8th Cir. 1989).

15 *Id.* at 201 ("Plaintiff was apprehended in the Hy-Vee lot adjacent to the shopping center after he fled from the store and from police. The police report indicated plaintiff possessed not only the stolen credit card of Richard Baker, but also (1) a credit card belonging to Henry Stronenger, (2) a credit card belonging to Carl Womble, (3) a credit card belonging to Kent Dann, (4) a Texas driver's license in the name of Steven Martin, and (5) a New York driver's license in the name of Harold Raphmond. In addition, plaintiff's car contained over $275.00 worth of purchases which had been made with Richard Baker's stolen credit card.").

16 *Id.*

17 *Id.*

18 *Id.* (explaining that the faculty felt taking Warren back "would be inconsistent with the duty of the Law School to the public and with the standards for admission to the Law School. Furthermore, such readmission would have a detrimental effect on the morale of the student body and would be detrimental to the reputation and standing of the Law School.").

19 *Id.* at 201-02.

20 *Id.* at 202.

21 *Id.*

22 *Id.* at 203 (footnote omitted).

23 No. 093149, 1991 WL 172863 (Conn. Super Ct. Aug. 28, 1991).

24 *Id.* at *1. Although the court does not identify Czarsty's crime, other sources explain that he was part of a local counterfeiting ring. *See, e.g., Agent Testifies About Trail of Counterfeit $20 Bills*, HARTFORD COURANT, Mar. 17, 1988, at C11.

25 *See Czarsty*, 1991 WL 172863, at *1.

26 *Id.*

27 *Id.* at *3. It is not known what happened to Czarsty's lawsuit. Prior to entering law school, Czarsty had opened a junkyard and it appears he continued to run it after his expulsion. *See Woodbury Auto Salvage, Inc.*, CT.Gov, *at* https://service.ct.gov/business/s/onlinebusinesssearch?language=en_US (last visited Apr. 1, 2022) (under filing number 0156476) (indicating that the business was incorporated in 1984 and administratively dissolved in 2019).

28 310 F. Supp. 2d 1256 (S.D. Fla. 2004), *later proceedings at* No. 03-20652-Civ-Lenard, No. 03-20652-Civ-Simonton, 2004 WL 2980711 (S.D. Fla. Dec. 17, 2004), *and later proceedings at* No. 03-20652-Civ-Lenard/Klein, 2005 WL 8154066 (S.D. Fla. Aug. 24, 2005), *aff'd*, 210 F. App'x 895, No. 05-15406, 2006 WL 3635409 (11th Cir. Dec. 13, 2006).

29 *Jarzynka*, 2005 WL 8154066, at *2-3.

30 *Id.* at *5.

31 *See Jarzynka*, 2004 WL 2980711, at *4 (partially granting plaintiff's motion to compel discovery responses); *Jarzynka*, 310 F. Supp. 2d at 1270 (partially granting defendants' motion to dismiss amended complaint).

32 *Jarzynka*, 2005 WL 8154066, at *5.

33 *Id.* at *9.

34 *Jarzynka*, 2006 WL 3635409, at *1. In 2009, Jarzynka self-published a book called *Blessed with Bipolar* and later became a talk radio host. *See Blessed with Bipolar—The Richard Jarzynka Show*, BLOG TALK RADIO, *at* https://www.blogtalkradio.com/bwb (last visited Apr. 1, 2022) (quoting Jarzynka as saying: "If you could pick which mental illness to have, Bipolar would be the only sane choice!").

35 No. G033813, 2004 WL 2669314, at *1 (Cal. Ct. App. Nov. 23, 2004), *later proceedings at* Nos. G034772 and G035515, 2006 WL 2773475 (Cal. Ct. App. Sept. 28, 2006), *cert. denied*, 552 U.S. 841 (2007).

36 *Taranto*, 2006 WL 2773475, at *1. In an earlier opinion, the court described Taranto's behavior in detail:

> Several students observed Taranto on one occasion in which no one was around, yet he "appeared to be talking to air." Students became frightened to sit near Taranto, and some avoided classes with him altogether. In one particular incident during a torts class, Taranto shouted repeatedly toward the back of the room, "'poor thing'" and "'do you want to take it outside'. . . ." He claimed he was responding to a student who directed the comment, "'poor thing,'" at him and that he simply asked the student to "'take it outside,'" but a witness perceived the exchange as a threat, noting Taranto displayed extreme agitation, clenching both his teeth and fists. Another student was so alarmed by the outburst that he contacted campus security. Responding, the security officer spotted Taranto laughing to himself as he drove off the campus.

Taranto, 2004 WL 2669314, at *1.

37 *Taranto*, 2006 WL 2773475, at *1.

38 *Id.*

39 *See* Taranto v. Stride & Assocs., Inc., No. G030731, 2003 WL 21153353 (Cal. Ct. App. May 20, 2003). The appeals court also resurrected Taranto's claims against a second employment agency called Contractors Tradecorps, Inc. *See id.* at *1.

40 *See Taranto*, 2004 WL 2669314, at *3.

41 In 2017, Whittier College decided to close the law school. *See* Sonali Kohli et al., *Law Students Caught Off Guard: Whittier College Will Close Affiliated School in Costa Mesa Amid Financial Struggles*, L.A. TIMES, Apr. 21, 2017, at B1 (explaining that the law school had been under ABA scrutiny for years due to its low bar pass rate).

42 *See Taranto*, 2006 WL 2773475, at *1.

43 *Id.* at *6.

44 *Id.* at *1.

45 *Id.* at *4-7. Taranto currently lists himself as a "construction professional." *See Bradley Taranto*, LINKEDIN, *at* https://www.linkedin.com/in/bradley-taranto-469b1ab4/ (last visited Apr. 1, 2022).

46 Civil Action No. 18-6880, 2020 WL 1030844 (E.D. La. Mar. 3, 2020).

47 There also are Loyola law schools in Chicago and Los Angeles. *See* American Bar Association, *List of ABA-Approved Law Schools in Alphabetical Order, at* https://www.americanbar.org/groups/legal_education/resources/aba_approved_law_schools/in_alphabetical_order/ (last visited Apr. 1, 2022).

48 *See Doe*, 2020 WL 1030844, at *1. The university's Board of Review based its decision to expel Doe on the following facts:

> Dating Violence – there was a preponderance of evidence that Mr. John Doe abused Ms. Jane Roe 2 both physically and sexually. This

decision was based on her statements, photos, and evidence submitted to the courts to obtain the restraining order.

Persistence Misconduct – this is the second offense of this same type of complaint within the year.

Conduct Unbecoming of a Loyola Student – in addition to persistence misconduct, he was also arrested which is in violation of his disciplinary probation.

Id. at *3.

49 *Id.* at *3-4.

50 *Id.* at *9.

51 No. 21-cv-00267, 2021 WL 1812891 (E.D. Ill. May 6, 2021).

52 *Id.* at *2.

53 *Id.* at *2-3.

54 *Id.* at *1.

55 *Id.* at *5. In January 2022, Syed filed a 344-page second amended complaint. *See* Lauraann Wood, *Northwestern Slams Ex-Law Student's 'Frivolous' Bias Suit*, Law360, Mar. 4, 2022, *at* https://www.law360.com/articles/1470972/northwestern-slams-ex-law-student-s-frivolous-bias-suit.

Chapter 8

CONCLUSION

As the foregoing chapters make clear, it is virtually impossible for an expelled law student to win a reinstatement lawsuit on the merits. Given this fact, such students do much better when they put their time and energy into pursuing a different vocation. But considering the shame that accompanies being expelled from law school,[1] coupled with what usually is an unshakeable (but incorrect) belief that they have been wronged and will be able to turn things around if given another chance, it is not hard to understand what motivates expelled law students to sue.[2] Accordingly, law schools should continue to brace for these kinds of lawsuits.[3]

1   *See supra* note 2 of Chapter 1.

2   For an interesting discussion of the medical reasons that cause some people to insist on suing even when there is no hope of winning, see C. Adam Coffey et al., *I'll See You in Court . . . Again: Psychopathology and Hyperlitigious Litigants*, 45 J. Am. Acad. Psychiatry *&* L. 62 (2017), *available at* http://jaapl.org/content/jaapl/45/1/62.full.pdf.

3   Just a day after the research for this book closed, Charlie Li, a former Willamette University law student, went public regarding her fight to be readmitted and told a reporter she planned to sue the school. See Meerah Powell, *International Student at Willamette Law School Alleges She was Expelled Due to Disability Discrimination*, OPB (Or. Pub. Broad.), Mar. 1, 2022, *at* https://www.opb.org/article/2022/03/01/willamette-university-college-of-law-student-honor-code-dismissal-disability-discrimination/. While Li claims she was expelled due to her medical disabilities, Willamette insists she was dismissed after being found guilty of violating the school's honor code and threatening a classmate. *Id.*

A short time after Li's story came to light, W. Stephen Lush II, who in 2004 was expelled from Northern Illinois University's law school for poor grades, had his long-running federal lawsuit against the school dismissed by the Seventh Circuit. *See* Lush v. Board of Trs. of N. Ill. Univ., 29 F.4th 377 (7th Cir. 2022), *rehearing denied*, No. 21-1394, 2022 WL 1088997 (7th Cir. Apr. 11, 2022). *See also* Lauraann Wood, *7th Circ. Tosses Ex-Law School Student's ADA Suit*, Law360, Mar. 29, 2022, *at* https://www.law360.com/articles/1478732/7th-circ-tosses-ex-law-school-student-s-ada-suit. Lush's similar state lawsuit was dismissed by the Illinois Supreme Court in 2020. *See* Lush v. Northern Ill. Univ. Coll. of L., 154 N.E.3d 772 (Ill. 2020).

Lastly, in Abo-Saif v. Board of Trs. of Univ. of Ill., No. 1-21-1091, 2022 WL 2350422 (Ill. App. Ct. June 30, 2022), a 2020 disability discrimination lawsuit brought by a John Marshall Law School student who was dismissed for poor grades was determined, due to the state's 2018 purchase of the school, to require re-filing in the court of claims.

TABLE OF CASES

L

M

Q

Quern v. Jordan, 153

R

Radcliff v. Landau, 80
Raiser v. Casserly, 63
Raiser v. San Diego County, 63
Raiser v. Ventura College of Law, 56, 62
Richter v. Catholic University of America, 109
Rittenhouse v. Board of Trustees of Southern Illinois University, 25
Robinson v. Hamline University, 83
Rollins v. Wyrick, 38
Rosenberg v. Golden Gate University, Inc., 91
Rothman v. Emory, 12

S

Sage v. CUNY Law School, 84
Salvador v. Touro College & University System, 31
Scott v. Western State University College of Law, 88
Shapiro v. Abraham Lincoln University School of Law, 101
Shields v. School of Law, Hofstra University, 74
Shinabargar v. Board of Trustees of the University of the District of
    Columbia, 36
Shuman v. University of Minnesota Law School, 17
Smith v. University of Detroit, 24
State *ex rel.* Duffel v. Marks, 31
Susan M. v. New York Law School, 79, 117
Syed v. Northwestern University, 166

T

U

V

W

Y

Z

John F. Kennedy University, 106, 137

University of Bridgeport, 79, 117-18, 163

   See also Quinnipiac University (this heading)

University of California

   Berkeley, 26

   Hastings College of the Law, 87

   Los Angeles, 5, 20

University of Colorado, 31

University of Dayton, 35, 95

University of Denver, 39

University of Detroit, 24

University of Exeter (England), 44

University of Georgia, 22

University of Hawaii, 168

University of Illinois, 37, 179

University of Kansas, 56

University of Kentucky, 40

University of La Verne, 15, 20

University of Louisiana, 31

University of Louisville, 40, 84, 149, 157

University of Maryland, 3, 23

University of Massachusetts, 29-30

University of Miami, 60

University of Michigan, 31

University of Minnesota, 17, 47-48

University of Mississippi, 168, 169

University of Missouri, 38

University of Montana, 72, 168

University of Nebraska, 146-47

University of New Hampshire, 36-37, 122

   See also Franklin Pierce Law Center (this heading)

University of North Dakota, 39, 57, 64

University of Oklahoma, 7, 23, 67

University of Pennsylvania, 26

LAW STUDENTS

CPSIA information can be obtained
at www.ICGtesting.com
Printed in the USA
JSHW042034090523
41494JS00001B/12